MANHOOD FOR AMATEURS

The Pleasures and Regrets of

MANHOOD FOR AMATEURS

a Husband, Father, and Son

Michael Chabon

HARPER

An Imprint of HarperCollins*Publishers*
www.harpercollins.com

HarperCollins books may be purchased for educational, business, or sales promotional use. For information, please write: Special Markets Department, HarperCollins Publishers, 10 East 53rd Street, New York, NY 10022.

Acknowledgment is made to the following, in which the essays in this collection first appeared, some differently titled or in a slightly different form: *Details*: "The Losers' Club," "William and I," "The Cut," "D.A.R.E.," "The Memory Hole," "The Binding of Isaac," "To the Legoland Station," "Hypocritical Theory," "The Splendors of Crap," "The Story of Our Story," "The Ghost of Irene Adler," "The Heartbreak Kid," "Faking It," "Art of Cake," "I Feel Good About My Murse," "Burning Women," "Verging," "Looking for Trouble," "Like, Cosmic," "Subterranean," "X09," "The Amateur Family," "Surefire Lines," "Cosmodemonic," "Boyland," "A Textbook Father," "Getting Out," "Radio Silence," "Normal Time," "X-mas," "Sky and Telescope," and "Daughter of the Commandment"; *Vogue*: "The Hand on My Shoulder"; the *New York Times Magazine*: "A Gift"; the *New York Times*: "On Canseco"; *Swing*: "Fever"; *Allure*: "A Woman of Valor." "The Wilderness of Childhood" was not previously published.

FIRST EDITION

Book design by Jennifer Daddio/Bookmark Design & Media Inc.

Library of Congress Cataloging-in-Publication Data
Chabon, Michael.
Manhood for amateurs : the pleasures and regrets of a husband, father, and son / Michael Chabon. – 1st ed.
p.   cm.
ISBN: 978-0-06-149018-7
1. Chabon, Michael—Marriage. 2. Chabon, Michael—Family. 3. Men—United States—Biography. 4. Husbands—United States—Biography. 5. Fathers—United States—Biography. 6. Sons—United States—Biography. 7. Marriage—United States. 8. Fatherhood—United States. 9. Masculinity—United States. 10. Authors, American—Biography. I. Title.
PS3553.H15Z463 2009
813'.54—dc22

[B]   2009004749

09 10 11 12 13   ID/RRD   10 9 8 7 6 5 4 3 2 1

To Steve Chabon

Anything worth doing is worth doing badly.

—G.K. CHESTERTON

Contents

[III]
STRATEGIES FOR THE FOLDING OF TIME

[IV]
EXERCISES IN MASCULINE AFFECTION

[V]
STYLES OF MANHOOD

CONTENTS

[VI]
ELEMENTS OF FIRE

[VII]
PATTERNS OF EARLY ENCHANTMENT

[VIII]
STUDIES IN PINK AND BLUE

[IX]
TACTICS OF WONDER AND LOSS

[X]
CUE THE MICKEY KATZ

[1]

SECRET HANDSHAKE

The Losers' Club

I typed the inaugural newsletter of the Columbia Comic Book Club on my mother's 1960 Smith Corona, modeling it on the monthly "Stan's Soapbox" pages through which Stan Lee created and sustained the idea of Marvel Comics fandom in the sixties and early seventies. I wrote it in breathless homage, rich in exclamation points, to Lee's prose style, that intoxicating smart-ass amalgam of Oscar Levant, Walter Winchell, Mad magazine, and thirty-year-old U.S. Army slang. Doing the typeset and layout with nothing but the carriage return (how old-fashioned that term sounds!), the tabulation key, and a gallon of Wite-Out, I divided my newsletter into columns and sidebars, filling each one with breezy accounts of the news, proceedings, and ongoing projects of the C.C.B.C. These included an announcement of the first meeting of the club. The meeting would be open to the public, with the price of admission covering enrollment.

For a fee of twenty-five dollars, my mother rented me a multipurpose room in the Wilde Lake Village Center, and I placed an advertisement in the local newspaper, the Columbia *Flier*. On the appointed Saturday, my mother drove me to the Village Center. She helped me set up a long conference table, surrounding it with a dozen and a half folding chairs. There were more tables ready if I needed them, but I didn't kid myself. One would probably be enough. I had lettered a sign, and we taped it to the door. It read: COLUMBIA COMIC BOOK CLUB. MEMBERSHIP/ADMISSION $1.

Then my mother went off to run errands, leaving me alone in the big, bare, linoleum-tiled multipurpose room. Half the room was closed off by an accordion-fold door that might, should the need arise, be collapsed to give way to multitudes. I sat behind a stack of newsletters and an El Producto cash box, ready to preside over the fellowship I had called into being.

In its tiny way, this gesture of baseless optimism mirrored the feat of Stan Lee himself. In the early sixties, when "Stan's Soapbox" began to apostrophize Marvel fandom, there was no such thing as Marvel fandom. Marvel was a failing company, crushed, strangled, and bullied in the marketplace by its giant rival, DC. Creating "The Fantastic Four"—the first "new" Marvel title— with Jack Kirby was a last-ditch effort by Lee, a mad flapping of the arms before the barrel sailed over the falls.

But in the pages of the Marvel comic books, Lee behaved from the start as if a vast, passionate readership awaited each issue that he and his key collaborators, Kirby and Steve Ditko, churned out. And in a fairly short period of time, this chutzpah—as in all those accounts of magical chutzpah so beloved by solitary boys like me—was rewarded. By pretending to have a vast network of fans, former fan Stanley Leiber found himself in possession of a vast network of fans. In conjuring, out of typewriter ribbon and folding chairs, the C.C.B.C., I hoped to accomplish a similar alchemy. By pretending to have friends, maybe I could invent some.

This is the point, to me, where art and fandom coincide. Every work of art is one half of a secret handshake, a challenge that seeks the password, a heliograph flashed from a tower window, an act of hopeless optimism in the service of bottomless longing. Every great record or novel or comic book convenes the first meeting of a fan club whose membership stands forever at one but which maintains chapters in every city—in every cranium—in the world. Art, like fandom, asserts the possibility of fellowship in a world built entirely from the materials of solitude. The novelist, the cartoonist, the songwriter, knows that the gesture is doomed from the beginning but makes it anyway, flashes his or her bit of mirror, not on the chance that the signal will be seen or understood but as if such a chance existed.

After I had been sitting at that big empty conference table for what felt like quite a long time, the door opened and a woman stuck her head in. I can still see her in my memory: her short blond hair parted in the center, her eyes metering the depth and density of the room, the tug of disappointment at the corners of her mouth.

"Oh," she said, seeing how things were with the Columbia Comic Book Club.

A moment later, her son pushed past her into the room. He was a kid about my age, blond like his mother, skinny, maybe a little girlish. For a moment he stared at me as if I puzzled him. Then he gazed up at his mother. She put her hands on his shoulders.

"I have a newsletter," I said at last, sliding the stack across the table.

The woman hesitated, then urged her son toward me, figuring or hoping, I suppose, that something could be salvaged, some kind of club business transacted. But the boy pushed back. That multipurpose room was not anywhere he wanted to be. God knows what kind of Araby he had erected, what fabulous tents he had pitched, in his own imagination of the event. A wordless argument followed, conducted by the bones of his shoulders and the fingers of her hands. At last she gave in to the force of his disappointment or to the barrage of failure rays that were pouring from the kid across the room.

"One dollar," she said seriously, considering the sign I had taped to the door with the same kind of black electrician's tape that was holding my eyeglasses together. "I think that might be a little too much for us."

I don't remember what kind of shape I was in when my own mother returned, or how she comforted me. I was a stoical kid, even an inexpressive one, given to elaborate displays of shrugging things off. In looking back at that day, I see now how much the brief existence of the C.C.B.C. had to do with mothers and sons, what a huge, even overwhelming maternal task is implied by that worn-out word *encouragement*. In spite of whatever consolation my mother may have offered, that was the moment when I began to think of myself as a failure. It's a habit I never lost. Anyone who has ever received a bad review knows how it outlasts, by decades, the memory of a favorable word. In my heart, to this day, I am always sitting at a big table in a roomful of chairs, behind a pile of errors, lies, and exclamation points, watching an empty doorway. My story and my stories are all, in one way or another, the same, tales of solitude and the grand pursuit of connection, of success and the inevitability of defeat.

Though I derive a sense of strength and confidence from writing and from my life as a husband and father, those pursuits are notoriously subject to endless setbacks and the steady exposure of shortcoming, weakness, and insufficiency—in particular in the raising of children. A father is a man who fails every day. Sometimes things work out: Your flashed message is received and read, your song is rerecorded by another band and goes straight to No. 1, your son blesses the memory of the day you helped him arrange the empty chairs of his foredoomed dream, your act of last-ditch desperation sends your comic-book company to the top of the industry. Success, however, does nothing to diminish the knowledge that failure stalks everything you do. But you always knew that. Nobody gets past the age of ten without that knowledge. Welcome to the club.

[II]

TECHNIQUES OF BETRAYAL

William and I

The handy thing about being a father is that the historic standard is so pitifully low. One day a few years back I took my youngest son to the market around the corner from our house in Berkeley, California, a town where, in my estimation, fathers generally do a passable job, with some fathers having been known to go a little overboard. I was holding my twenty-month-old in one arm and unloading the shopping cart onto the checkout counter with the other. I don't remember what I was thinking about at the time, but it is as likely to have been the original 1979 jingle for Honey Nut Cheerios or nothing at all as it was the needs, demands, or ineffable wonder of my son. I wasn't quite sure why the woman in line behind us—when I became aware of her—kept beaming so fondly in our direction. She had on rainbow leggings, and I thought she might be a little bit crazy and therefore fond of everyone.

"You are such a good dad," she said finally. "I can tell."

I looked at my son. He was chewing on the paper coating of a wire twist tie. A choking hazard, without a doubt; the wire could have pierced his lip or tongue. His hairstyle tended to the cartoonier pole of the Woodstock-Einstein continuum. His face was probably a tad on the smudgy side. Dirty, even. One might have been tempted to employ the word *crust*.

"Oh, this isn't my child," I told her. "I found him in the back."

Actually, I thanked her. I went off with my boy in one arm and a bag of groceries in the other, and when we got home I put a plastic bowl filled with Honey Nut Cheerios in front of him and checked my e-mail. I was a really good dad.

I don't know what a woman needs to do to impel a perfect stranger to inform her in the grocery store that she is a really good mom. Perhaps perform an emergency tracheotomy with a Bic pen on her eldest child while simultaneously nursing her infant and buying two weeks' worth of healthy but appealing breaktime snacks for the entire cast of Lion King, Jr. In a grocery store, no mother is good or bad; she is just a mother, shopping for her family. If she wipes her kid's nose or tear-stained cheeks, if she holds her kid tight, entertains her kid's nonsensical claims, buys her kid the organic non-GMO whole-grain version of Honey Nut Cheerios, it adds no useful data to our assessment of her. Such an act is statistically insignificant. Good mothering is not measurable in a discrete instant, in an hour spent rubbing a baby's gassy belly, in the braiding of a tangled mass of morning hair. Good mothering is a long-term pattern, a lifelong trend of behaviors most of which go unobserved at the time by anyone, least of all the mother herself. We do not judge mothers by snapshots but by years of images painstakingly accumulated from the orbit-ing satellite of memory. Once a year, maybe, and on certain fatal birthdays, and at our weddings or her funeral, we might collate all the available data, analyze it, and offer our irrefutable judgment: good mother.

In the intervals—just ask my wife—all mothers are (in their own view) bad. Because the paradoxical thing, or one of the para-doxical things, about the low standard to which fathers are held (with the concomitant minimal effort required to exceed the standard and win the sobriquet of "good dad") is that your basic garden-variety mother, not only working hard at her own end of the child-rearing enterprise (not to mention at her actual job) but so often taxed with the slack from the paternal side of things, tends in my experience to see her career as one of perennial insuf-ficiency and self-doubt. This is partly because mothers are attuned, in a way that most fathers have a hard time managing, to the spec-ter of calamity that haunts their children. Fathers are popularly supposed to serve as protectors of their children, but in fact men lack the capacity for identifying danger except in the most narrow spectrum of the band. It is women—mothers—whose organs of anxiety can detect the vast invisible flow of peril through which their children are obliged daily to make their way. The father on a camping trip who manages to beat a rattlesnake to death with a can of Dinty Moore in a tube sock may rest for decades on the en-suing laurels yet somehow snore peacefully every night beside his sleepless wife, even though he knows perfectly well that the Polly Pocket toys may be tainted with lead-based paint, and the Rite-

Aid was out of test kits, and somebody had better go order them online, overnight delivery, even though it is four in the morning. It is in part the monumental open-endedness of the job, with its infinite number of infinitely small pieces, that routinely leads mothers to see themselves as inadequate, therefore making the task of recognizing their goodness, at any given moment, so hard.

I know there's a double standard at work; I suppose if I'm honest, I would have to acknowledge that in my worst moments, I'm grateful for it, for the easy credit that people—*mothers*, for God's sake—are willing to extend to me for doing very little at all. It's like pulling into a parking space with a nickel in your pocket to find that somebody left you an hour's worth of quarters in the meter. This double standard has been in place for a long time now, though over the past few decades a handful of items—generally having to do with cooking and caring for babies—have been added to the list of minimum expectations for a good father. My father, more or less like all the men of his era, class, and cultural background, went for a certain amount of spasmodically enthusiastic fathering, parachuting in from time to time with some new pursuit or project, engaging like an overweening superpower in a program of parental nation-building in the far-off land of his children before losing interest or running out of emotional capital and leaving us once more to the regime of our mother, a kind of ancient, all-pervasive folkway, a source of attention and control and structure so reliable as to be imperceptible, like the air. My father educated me in appreciating the things he appreciated, and in ridiculing those he found laughable, and in disbelieving the things he found dubious. When I was a small boy, tractable and respectful and preternaturally adult, with my big black glasses and careful phraseology, he would take me on house calls and at-home insurance physicals along with his stethoscope and Taylor hammer. When he was done being a father for the time being, he would leave me in my corner of his life, tucked into the black bag of his affections. At night sometimes, if he made it home from the hospital, he would come in and lean down and brush my soft cheek with his scratchy one.

If the lady in the rainbow tights had seen us walking down a street in Phoenix, Arizona, in 1966, with me swinging my plastic doctor bag full of candy pills and deneedled hypos and trying to match my stride to his, she probably would have told him that he was a good dad, too. And she would not have been saying very much less or more than she was saying to me.

My father, born in the gray-and-silver Movietone year of 1938, was part of the generation of Americans who, in their twenties and thirties, approached the concepts of intimacy, of authenticity and open emotion, with a certain tentative abruptness, like people used to automatic transmission learning how to drive a stick shift. They wanted intimacy, but they were not sure how far they could trust it to take them. My father didn't hug me a lot or kiss me. I don't remember holding his hand past the age of three or four. When I got older and took an interest in the art of becoming a grown-up, it proved hard to find other, nonphysical kinds of intimacy with him. He didn't like to share his anxieties about his work, relationships, or life, rarely took me into his confidence, never dared to admit the deepest intimacy of all—that he didn't know what the hell he was doing.

In 1974 I saw a musical cartoon called "William's Doll." It was a segment in that echt-seventies, ungrammatically titled children's television special created by Marlo Thomas, *Free to Be You and Me.* The segment, based on a book by Charlotte Zolotow, was about a boy who begs his bemused parents to buy him a baby doll, a request to which they are nonplussed if not, in the case of William's father, outright hostile. William is mocked, scolded, and bullied for his desire, and his parents try to bribe him out of it. But William persists, and in the end his wise grandmother overrules his father and buys him a doll.

Even as a boy of ten, I could feel the radical nature of the mode of being a father that "William's Doll" was holding out to me:

William wants a doll

So that when he has a baby someday

He'll learn how to dress it

Put diapers on double

And gently caress it

To bring up a bubble

And care for his baby

Like every good father should learn to do.

I was moved by the sight of the animated William reveling, grooving, in the presence of the baby doll that his grandmother placed in his waiting arms. There was a promise in the song and the sight of him of a different way of being a father, a physical, quiet, tender, and quotidian way free of projects and agendas, and there was a suggestion that this way was something not merely possible or commendable but long-desired. Something was missing from William's life before his grandmother stepped in and bought him a doll, and by implication, something was missing from the life of William's father, and of my father, and of all the other men who were not allowed to play with dolls. Every time I listened to the song on the record album, I felt the lack in myself and in my father.

My dad did what was expected of him, but like most men of the time, he didn't do very much apart from the traditional winning of bread. He didn't take me to get my hair cut or my teeth cleaned; he didn't make the appointments. He didn't shop for my clothes. He didn't make my breakfast, lunch, or dinner. My mother did all of those things, and nobody ever told her when she did them that it made her a good mother.

The fact of the matter is that—and fuck the woman in the rainbow tights for her compliment—there's nothing I work harder at than being a good father, unless it's being a good husband, which doesn't come any easier but tends not to get remarked on when I'm standing in line at the supermarket. I cook and clean, do the dishes, get the kids to their appointments, etc. Many times over, I have lived entire days whose only leitmotifs were the vomitus and excrement of my offspring and whose only plot was the removal and disposal thereof. I have made their Halloween costumes and baked their birthday cakes and prepared a dozen trays of my mother-in-law's garlic chicken wings for class potlucks because last names starting with A–F had to bring the hors d'oeuvres. In other words, I define being a good father in precisely the same terms that we ought to define being a good mother—doing my part to handle and stay on top of the endless parade of piddly shit. And like good mothers all around the world, I fail every day in my ambition to do the work, to make it count, to think ahead and hang in there through the tedium and really see, really feel, all the pitfalls that threaten my children, rattlesnakes included. How could I not fail when I can check out any time I want to and know that my wife will still be there making those dentist appointments and ensuring that there's a wrapped, age-appropriate birthday present for next Saturday's pool party? All I need to do is hold my kid in the checkout line—all I need to do is stick around—and the world will crown me and favor me with smiles.

So, all right, it isn't fair. But the truth is that I don't want to be a good father out of egalitarian feminist principles. Those principles—though I cherish them—are only the means to an end for me.

The daily work you put into rearing your children is a kind of intimacy, tedious and invisible as mothering itself. There is another kind of intimacy in the conversations you may have with your children as they grow older, in which you confess to failings, reveal anxieties, share your bouts of creative struggle, regret, frustration. There is intimacy in your quarrels, your negotiations and running jokes. But above all, there is intimacy in your contact with their bodies, with their shit and piss, sweat and vomit, with their stubbled kneecaps and dimpled knuckles, with the rips in their underpants as you fold them, with their hair against your lips as you kiss the tops of their heads, with the bones of their shoulders and with the horror of their breath in the morning as they pursue the ancient art of forgetting to brush. Lucky me that I should be permitted the luxury of choosing to find the intimacy inherent in this work that is thrust upon so many women. Lucky me.

The Cut

I f you are a Jew, eight days after your son is born, you hand him
to a man with a scalpel, and the man uses his fine instrument
to cut off a small piece of your new baby. It is for this reason,
though you will have to take my word on the matter, that my penis
has no prepuce, or foreskin: My parents voluntarily had it sliced
off by a little old guy with a sharp blade when I was eight days old.
The same procedure was performed at the same age on my father,
and on my grandfathers, all of whom were in attendance that afternoon, and on their fathers and grandfathers, stretching back to
the time when knives were shards of obsidian or flint. The stated
reason for this minutely savage custom is that God—the God of
Abraham—commanded it.

That is not an argument that ought to hold a lot of water with
me. I have confused ideas of deity, heavily influenced by mind-
altering years of reading science fiction, that do not often trouble me, but one thing I know for certain, and have known since
the age of five or six, is that I really can't stand the God of Abra-

ham. In fact, I consider Him to constitute the pattern to which every true asshole I have ever known in my life has pretty well conformed. In His infinite capacity to engineer and experience disappointment, in His arbitrary and capricious cruelty, and in the evident pleasure He derives from the exercise thereof, there is probably a sharp insight into the nature of fathers generally, since at one time or another, if not on a daily basis, each of us fathers is the biggest asshole in the world. Or else the God of Abraham is a metaphor, crude but effective, for the caprice, brutality, and disappointment of life itself. I don't know. In any case, nothing having to do with this particular version of God and His supposed Commandments could ever satisfactorily explain my willingness to subject my sons, of which I have two fine examples, to mutilation: the only honest name for this raw act that my wife and I have twice invited men with knives to come into our house and perform, in the presence of all our friends and family, with a nice buffet and a Weekend Cake from Just Desserts.

"Why are we doing this again?" my wife asked me, not for the first time, on the night of the seventh day of our second son's life.

We were in bed, sitting up against the headboard, semi-comatose, dazzled by sleeplessness in a way that felt shared and almost pleasurable. The baby was at her breast, working his jaw, the nipple impossibly huge in his astonished little mouth. I leaned my shoulder against my wife's, and she laid her head against my cheek, and together our bodies formed a kind of cupped palm around the baby in her arms. The lamp clipped to the headboard enclosed us in a circle of soft light. I doubt that any rational observer could have inferred from that intimate huddle, from the shelter we had formed of ourselves, the date we had made for the baby and his foreskin at one o'clock the following afternoon.

"I guess," she said, attempting to answer her own question, "he ought to match his big brother."

"I guess," I said, recognizing this as a variant of a common justification advanced by Jews inclined, in most other respects, to disregard the Commandments of the God of Abraham: that it would somehow disturb or gravely puzzle a child to contemplate the difference in appearance between his own hooded penis and his father's peeled one. Possibly it might hang him up about penises in general. In turn this might lead, via unspecified, possibly mythical, psychological processes, to some kind of sexual dysfunction, oedipal collapse, Kafkaesque problems with authority. . . . That part of the argument tended to get left to the imagination. It was usually enough to intone the reasonable principle that a son ought genitally to match his father in order to evoke a cognizant nod of the head in the listener—a spouse, a gentile friend, a gentile spouse. I knew this matching-penises argument was a favorite among interfaith couples, frequently advanced by the non-Jewish partner as she attempted to get her mind around the idea of letting some nut with a scalpel come after her baby's little thing.

"But who knows?" I continued. "None of their other parts have to match. They could have different eye color, different hair, different noses, differently shaped heads. One of them could have a fissured tongue or a rudimentary third nipple." I have a rudimentary third nipple, which was why this particular example occurred to me. "What's the big deal about the penis? By the time this guy here gets old enough that he starts making a critical study of penises, he probably won't be seeing his brother's very often."

"Yeah," she said, letting the argument flutter to the ground like a losing lottery ticket.

We had been through all of the standard arguments—hygiene, cancer prevention, psychological fitness, the Zero Mostel tradition—the first time around, with our oldest son, and found that they are all debatable at best, while there is plenty of convincing evidence that sexual pleasure is considerably diminished by the absence of a foreskin. But I never know how to think about that one. It is like in *A Princess of Mars*, in which we are informed that on the red planet Barsoom they have nine colors in their spectrum and not seven; I have tried and failed many times to imagine those extra Barsoomian colors.

"What?" my wife asked, sensing my abstraction from the matter at hand.

"I was thinking about the Mars books of Edgar Rice Burroughs," I said glumly.

"Do they feature ritual genital mutilation?"

"Not that I recall."

The baby popped off the breast, and sighed, and considered one of the anemone wisps of drifting smoke, like the aftermath of a bursting skyrocket, that I imagined his thoughts to resemble. At seven days he gave evidence of a melancholy or even mournful nature. He sighed again, and so I sighed, thinking that we were about to confirm, in the worst possible way, all the lugubrious ideas about the world that he already seemed to have formed. Then he burrowed back in for another go at his mother.

"If it was a girl," my wife said, "we would never."

"Never."

We had been through this, all of this, before. Every time some brave doctor or grown victim spoke out against the ritual mutilation of girls' labias in certain subcultures, we were duly outraged.

"It's not one bit less barbaric than what they do over there," my wife said. "Not one."

"Agreed."

"It's madness. The more I think about it, the more insane it seems."

I said I thought that was probably true of everything our religion expected us to do, from burying a pot in the ground because one day a meatball accidentally rolled inside of it, to replacing the hair you had shaved off, out of modesty, with a fabulous-looking five-thousand-dollar wig. In fact, I said, most human social behavior probably fit the formula she had just proposed—for example, neckties. But my observation failed to impress or even, it seemed, to register with my wife. She was gazing down at our little boy with the eyes of a betrayer, filled with pity and tears.

"You have to at least promise me," she said, "that it's not going to hurt him."

As with the first time, we had shopped around the mohel market, looking for a guy who used, or would permit us to use, an anesthetic cream. Traditionally, the only painkiller was a drop of sweet wine introduced between the lips on the wine-soaked tip of a cloth, and a lot of mohelim stuck to that way of doing things. Some of them would suggest giving the boy Tylenol an hour beforehand. And then there were those who prescribed a cream such as Emla. The mohel who was coming tomorrow had given us complicated instructions that involved filling a bottle nipple with the Emla well before the procedure, then fitting it right over the penis, having first enlarged the hole in the tip of the nipple to permit the flow of urine. It was reassuring to think of the entire organ being immersed, steeped in numbing unguent, for hours beforehand. But even the absence of pain, if we could assure it, did not really detract from the fundamental brutality of the business.

"It's not going to hurt," I told her, though of course, having never immersed my entire penis in anesthetic cream and then subjected it to minor surgery, I had no idea whether it was going to hurt him or not. That was one of the skills you learned as a father fairly early on, and it had roots as ancient as whatever words Abraham had crafted to lure his son Isaac up that mountainside to the high place where he would bare his beloved child's breast to the heavens, as he had been commanded to do by the almighty asshole or by the god-shaped madness whose voice was rolling like thunder through his brain. It was not the making of a covenant that the rite called Brit Milah commemorated, but the betrayal of one. Because you promised your children, simply by virtue of having them, and thereafter a hundred times a day, that you would shield them, always and with all your might, from harm, from madness, from men with their knives and their bloody ideas. I supposed it was never too soon for them to start learning what a liar you were.

I reached down and stroked the baby's cheek.

"It's not going to hurt," I promised him, and he looked up at me, his gaze solemn and melancholy, without the slightest idea of what lay in store for him in this world but ready—born ready—to believe me.

One night when she was thirteen, my older daughter opened the discussion at dinner with something that had apparently been troubling her: a problem in the interpretation of rock lyrics. Since she saw the film *Across the Universe*, her interest in the Beatles had intensified, and lately, I had been fielding many such interpretative queries in my capacity as Senior Fellow in Beatle Studies—deciding whether or not, at the end of "Norwegian Wood," the singer burns down the girl's house because she makes him sleep in her bathtub; and working hard not to have to explain to my older son, not quite eleven at the time, what delectable treat was signified in Liverpool slang by the phrase "fish and finger pie." (So tasty that the singer orders four of them!)

"Dad," my daughter said, "when he goes 'I get high with a little help from my friends,' is he talking about getting high high? Or is he just saying that being around his friends makes him feel really, really, like, *happy*?"

The ten-year-old was at the kitchen counter pouring himself

a glass of milk, but in the instant that preceded my reply, without even looking his way, I could feel him training his detectors on me, his array of receiving dishes all swiveling in my direction. Every time somebody fired one up in a movie, the kid looked simultaneously troubled and intrigued by the sight. He is a clear thinker who likes his questions settled, and I had seen him wrestling for some time with the mixed messages our culture puts out about the pleasures and disasters of drug and alcohol use.

"High high," I said.

My daughter's cheeks colored as I met her gaze, in embarrassment and in pleasure, too, I thought, as though her insight had been confirmed in a way that gratified her sense of her own sophistication.

I could remember this moment in my own life, when I was exactly her age and had yet to encounter actual marijuana: the sudden consciousness, a flower of preteen lore and hermeneutics, that the lyrics to Beatles songs were salted with and in some cases constructed entirely from sly and overt references to drug use. Not just "Lucy in the Sky with Diamonds" or "She Said She Said," which supposedly re-creates an acid-powered conversation between John Lennon and Peter Fonda, but less obvious numbers like "Girl," on *Rubber Soul*, which was, it was claimed, a protracted allegory of marijuana use, with the hissed sighs that punctuate its choruses meant to represent the sound of someone taking a big, long toke. The line *Roll up for the mystery tour*, I had been told, referred to the rolling of joints.

So I recognized that flush in my daughter's cheeks. She was

a good girl, and I had once been a good boy, and I remembered that simultaneous sense of disapproval and fascination with the lyrical misbehavior of the boys from Liverpool. Thirteen is the age at which you begin to become fully aware of hypocrisy, contradiction, ambiguity, coded messages, subtexts; it is the age, therefore, at which you must begin to attempt to sort things out for yourself, to grab hold, if you can, of any shining thread in the dizzying labyrinth. And there, for me as for my children three decades later, were the Beatles, passing with astonishing and even brutal swiftness from the self-censoring radio-ready plaintext of "Love Me Do" and "I Wanna Hold Your Hand" to the encrypted thickets of songs like "I Am the Walrus" or "Happiness Is a Warm Gun": the eight-year chronicle in music of the band's attempt to sort things out for themselves as they came of age, the oeuvre itself a dazzling mass of puzzles and contradictions to be sorted.

"Dad, what does it feel like?" my son said, returning to the table with his glass of milk.

"Getting high?" I said. This time there was no hesitation. I had thought about this conversation, imagined it, planned for it, enough that I ought to have been ready; but even though I had spoken often with my wife (who for many years taught a class at Boalt Hall, UC Berkeley's law school, called "Legal and Social Implications of the War on Drugs") about our parental approach to talking about drug use, now that the moment was actually upon me (and she just happened to be out of town), I found that I was not ready at all. I was caught completely off guard. And maybe that's why I came right out with the truth.

"It feels pretty good," I said. "It makes you feel like you're really, uh, *being with* the people you're with. It makes you insanely hungry and thirsty. It makes you paranoid. It makes your heart race. It makes you sluggish. It makes you think things are really funny that might not actually be that funny at all."

"Like dead bodies?" my younger daughter suggested brightly. She was only six years old, but it looked like she was going to be in on this discussion, too.

"Uh, yeah, well, no, more like a bad Elvis movie," I said. "It makes you have thoughts that seem really, really deep and profound, and then the next day when you remember them, they seem totally lame."

"I wrote a poem in a dream I had," the thirteen-year-old said. "The same thing happened with that."

"Wait," the ten-year-old said. "Wait. You mean—have you actually *smoked* marijuana?"

Here it was, the big moment, the one we had all been waiting for, dreading, preparing for years in advance.

"Duh!" the thirteen-year-old informed her brother, doubling down on her proven-worldly views of the role of drugs in modern culture. "Like, every adult over a certain age has done it."

"Well, not every adult," I said. "But yes. I have."

"How many times?" my son said, eyes wide.

So far, even blindsided as I had been by the abrupt onset of this conversation, I hadn't violated the guiding principle my wife and I had decided on for its eventual proper conduct: I had been honest.

But now I had a moment's pause before replying, unwilling to pronounce those two simple words: *one million.*

The first person I ever saw smoking pot was my mother, sometime around 1977 or so, sitting in the front seat of her friend Kathy's car, passing a little metal pipe back and forth before we went in to see a movie at the Westview in Catonsville, Maryland. I have a dim sense that at fourteen I neither disapproved of nor felt any surprise at this behavior, leading me to conclude that my mother already must have told me, prepared me with the information, that she was "experimenting" with pot (because that was all it ever amounted to for her—a brief reagent test conducted within the beaker of her new status as a single woman in the great wild laboratory of the 1970s). If I was shocked by the idea of my mother breaking the law, that shock must have been mitigated by the casualness, and by the lack of shame or embarrassment with which my mother, an otherwise upright, sober, and law-abiding taxpayer, went about it. It appeared to be no big deal for a couple of grown women to smoke a bowl: an innocent, everyday sign of the times. Nevertheless, smoking marijuana remained for years afterward nothing I had any interest in trying myself, not so much because I feared its effects or even because it was against the law but simply because I was a good boy, and as such I looked down my nose with a cosmic, Galactus-sized censoriousness at the kids I knew—stoners, burnouts—who smoked it. I would not have minded breaking the law or getting high, but I could not abide the thought of being bad.

I clung to my increasingly cumbersome and ineffectual goodness, fighting a series of rearguard actions against the increasing presence in my life of rock and roll and sex, until, like the personnel of the U.S. embassy in Saigon leaping to the helicopters, I abandoned it entirely, at once. Early in October of my first term at Carnegie Mellon University, I was taught the rudiments of bong-handling by a team of experts. I lay down on the floor of a dorm room in Mudge Hall, under the light of a single red bulb, and swam through layers of warmth and well-being while an apparently infinite, starry, velvet-bright quantity of wonder was ladled into my ears by Jeff Beck, Jan Hammer and his spacefaring Group.

That was 1980. I smoked marijuana (with odd European forays into the mysteries of hashish) over the course of the next twenty years, never every day, mostly on weekends or when some came around, but at times with all the fierce passion of a true hobbyist. The price went up, and the quality improved so acutely that the nature of the high began to alter without quite changing, like a television picture increasing the resolution of its image. My level of dope-smoking peaked, becoming nearly habitual just after the breakup of my first marriage in 1990, and began to dwindle thereafter as the elevated concentrations of THC (or something) took a toll and I found that getting high often left me feeling apprehensive, hypercritical of myself, and prone to an unwelcome awareness of my life as nothing but a pile of botched and unfinished tasks. Over the course of these pot years I graduated from college, got a master's degree, wrote a number of novels, paid my bills and my taxes, etc. I was never arrested, never got into any kind of trouble, never broke anything that could not be repaired. Mostly it had been fun, sometimes hugely; sometimes not at all. Marijuana could intensify the sunshine of a perfect summer day, but it could also deepen the gloom of a wintry afternoon; it had bred false camaraderies and drawn my attention to deep flaws and fault lines when what mattered—what matters so often in the course of everyday human life—were the surfaces and the joins.

Be honest, my wife and I had agreed.

"I have smoked it a number of times," I told my son. "But I don't do it anymore."

This was true. Without ceremony or regret, I smoked marijuana for the last time in 2005—having not smoked any for at least a year before that—when I found myself, stoned out of my brain and very much not following the plot of Stephen Chow's *God of Cookery*, unexpectedly called upon to engage in some urgent full-on parenting: There was an abortive sleepover and a necessary stretch of late-night driving to be done. Though I somehow managed to pull it off, gripping the wheel, heart pounding, the world beyond the windshield as trackless and unfathomable as any Jeff Beck guitar solo, I spent the next hour fighting off the knowledge that I was not up to the task, and I vowed that I would never risk putting my children or myself in that position again. On some fundamental level, I was no longer willing to endure, or capable of enjoying, that kind of fun.

"Why did you stop?" those children wanted to know. "Because it's really illegal?"

"Well, it is really illegal," I agreed. "In some ways, a lot more illegal than it used to be when I was younger. But that's not really it. It has to do with, well, with being ready, you know. It's just not something I'm ready to do anymore. And it's not something you guys are ready to do, either. Right?"

"Right," they said at once, with all the firmness and certainty I would have mustered myself in those years before I sailed off into the red light and velvet darkness.

"The truth is," I told them, then pushed myself to live up to the principle my wife and I had established for contending not only with this issue but with all the other hypocrisies that life as a parent entails. *I want to tell you / My head is filled with things to say*, as George Harrison once sang, *When you're here / All those words, they seem to slip away.* "The truth is that I'm confused about what to tell you," I said. "But I mostly want us all to tell each other the truth."

They said that sounded all right to them and that I shouldn't worry. That's just what I would have said at their age.

The Memory Hole

Almost every school day, at least one of my four children comes home with art: a drawing, a painting, a piece of handicraft, a construction-paper assemblage, an enigmatic apparatus made from pipe cleaners, sparkles, and clay. And almost every bit of it ends up in the trash. My wife and I have to remember to shove the things down deep, lest one of the kids stumble across the ruin of his or her laboriously stapled paper-plate-and-dried-bean maraca wedged in with the junk mail and the collapsed packaging from a twelve-pack of squeezable yogurt. But there is so much of the stuff; we don't know what else to do with it. We don't toss all of it. We keep the good stuff—or what strikes us, in the Zen of that instant between scraping out the lunch box and sorting the mail, as good. As worthier somehow: more vivid, more elaborate, more accurate, more sweated over. A crayon drawing that fills the entire sheet of newsprint from corner to corner, a lifelike smile on the bill of a penciled flamingo. We stack the good stuff in a big drawer, and when the drawer is finally full, we pull out the stuff and stick it in a plastic bin that we keep in the attic. We never revisit it. We never get the children's artwork down and sort through it with them, the way we do with photo albums, and say "That's how you used to draw curly hair" or "See how you made your letter E's with seven crossbars?" I'm not sure why we're saving it except that getting rid of it feels so awful.

Under the curatorship of my mother, my brother's and my collected artwork is, if I may say so, a vastly more impoverished archive. From the years preceding high school there is almost nothing at all. The countless scenes of strafing Spitfires taking heavy German ack-ack fire, the corrugated-cardboard-and-foil George Washington hatchets, the clay menorahs (I never did make any dreidels out of clay), the works in crayon resist and papier-mâché and yarn and in media so mixed as to include Cheerios, autumn leaves, and dirt—gone, all of it. Do I care? Does it pain me to have lost forever this irrefutable evidence of my having been, if neither a prodigy nor an embryonic Matisse, a child? If my mother had held on to more of my childhood artwork, would I be happier now? Would the narrative that I have constructed of the nature and course of my childhood be more complete? I guess ultimately, I have no way of answering these questions. It's like wondering whether sex would be more pleasurable if I had not been worked over by that old Jew with a knife at the age of eight days. How much more pleasurable, really, do I need it to be?

When I run across one of the pieces of artwork that my mother did save—paintings that I made in my junior and senior years of high school, for the most part—the prevailing emotion I experience, with breathtaking vividness, is the acute discontent that I felt at the time of their creation, a dissatisfaction purified of any residual sense of pride or accomplishment. Their flaws of perspective and construction, the places where I cheated or fudged or simply could not pull something off, even a faint tempera-scented whiff of the general miasma of mortification and insufficiency in which I then swam—they all present themselves to my sight and recollection with a force that makes me a little ill.

I'm not trying to excuse the act of throwing away my children's artwork. The crookedest mark of a colored pencil on the back of a bank-deposit envelope, vaguely in the shape of a fish, is like a bright, stray trace of the boundless pleasure I take in watching my kids interact with the world. The set of processes joining their minds to their fingertips is a source of profound interest and endless speculation, a mystery that, through their artworks, my children endlessly expound. I know that if I live long enough, a time will come when their childhoods will strike me as having been mythically brief. Almost nothing will remain of these days, and they will be women and men, and I will look back on the lost piles of their drawings and paintings and sketches, the cubic yards of rubbings and scratchings consigned to the recycling bin, the reef's worth of shells, sand, and coral glued to their découpage souvenirs of vacations in Hawaii and Maine, and rue my barbarism. I will be haunted by the memory of the way my younger daughter looks at me when she chances upon a crumpled sheet of paper in the recycling bin, bearing the picture, the very portrait, of five minutes stolen from the headlong rush of their hour in my care: She looks betrayed.

"I don't know how that got in there," I tell her. "That was clearly a mistake. What a great dog."

"It's a girl kung fu master."

"Of course," I say. When she isn't looking, I throw it away again.

It's not only her artwork that I'm busy throwing away. Almost every hour that I spend with my children is disposed of just as surely, tossed aside, burned through like money by a man on a spree. The sum total of my clear memories of them—of their un-intended aphorisms, gnomic jokes, and the sad plain truths they have expressed about the world; of incidents of precociousness, Gothic madness, sleepwalking, mythomania, and vomiting; of the way light has struck their hair or eyelashes on vanished after-noons; of the stupefying tedium of games we have played on rainy Sundays; of highlights and horrors from their encyclopedic his-tory of odorousness; of the 297,000 minor kvetchings and heart-felt pleas I have responded to over the past eleven years with fury, tenderness, utter lack of interest, or a heartless and automatic compassion—those memories, when combined with the sum total of photographs that we have managed to take, probably add up, for all four of my children, to under 1 percent of everything that we have undergone, lived through, and taken pleasure in together.

The truth is that in every way, I am squandering the treasure of my life. It's not that I don't take enough pictures, though I don't, or that I don't keep a diary, though iCal and my monthly Visa bill are the closest I come to a thoughtful prose record of events. Every day is like a kid's drawing, offered to you with a strange mixture of ceremoniousness and offhand disregard, yours for the keeping. Some of the days are rich and complicated, others inscrutable, others little more than a stray gray mark on a ragged page. Some you manage to hang on to, though your reasons for doing so are often hard to fathom. But most of them you just ball up and throw away.

The Binding of Isaac

I was there, in Grant Park, on the night when Barack Obama began to shoulder all the possible meanings of his victory. You could hear it in his voice as the weight of it settled on him, and in the simple, judicious gravity of his language. You could see it in the glint, like the reflection of some awful or awesome vista, that lit his tired eyes. On a giant television screen to the right of the dais we could see what the world was seeing, and we could begin to imagine all the things that for Obama and for all of us were going to change henceforward. It was heady to contemplate, and thrilling, and after such a fierce and interminable campaign, there was also a tremendous sense of relief as we passed from the months of active wishing to this hour of having it be so. But among the most powerful emotions that stirred me as I stood there in the crowd, on that unseasonably warm evening with my son Abraham perched on my shoulders, was sadness. And that caught me a little unawares. I felt guilty about it. I knew I was only supposed to be happy at that moment, thrilled, grave, tired, relieved, duly awestruck—but happy. Yet I couldn't stop thinking about his two little girls.

Like the rest of the world, even many of those who had (by their own accounts the next morning) voted, connived, pontificated, or railed against Barack Obama, I held my breath as I watched him first walk out to the podium that night with Michelle, Malia, and Sasha. The four of them, dressed in shades of red and black, seemed to catch and hold a different kind of light, the light of history, astonishing and clear. Time stopped, and I was conscious as I have been very few times in my life—the morning of September 11, 2001, was, terribly, another—of seeing something that had never been seen. It was not only the beauty, or the blackness, or the youth of the new first family, or some combination of the three. It was the unmistakable air of mutual engagement the Obamas give off, the sense of being a fully operational—loving, struggling, seeking, adjusting, testing, playing, mythologizing, arguing, rationalizing, celebrating, compromising, affirming, denying—family. I felt that I had never seen a presidential family that was so clearly a working family in the sense of the everyday effort involved. When I was born, there were children in the White House, though they moved out, half orphaned, before I was six months old. I can remember Tricia Nixon's wedding, and Amy Carter and Chelsea Clinton getting braces or rolling Easter eggs on the White House lawn. But none of those families ever reminded me, ever seemed to reflect—at the fundamental level of daily operations where every great, august, well-reasoned principle and theory you profess or hold dear gets proved or shattered—my own.

With his daughters darting around his long legs, I saw Barack Obama as a father, like me. And I folded my hands behind my son's knobby back, to bolster him there on my shoulders, and gave his bottom a squeeze, and watched those radiant girls waving and smiling at the quarter-million of us, faces and voices and starry camera flashes, and thought *I would never have the nerve or the strength or the sense of mission or the grace or the cruelty to do that to you, kid*. There are no moments more painful for a parent than those in which you contemplate your child's perfect innocence of some imminent pain, misfortune, or sorrow. That innocence (like every kind of innocence children have) is rooted in their trust of you, one that you will shortly be obliged to betray; whether it is fair or not, whether you can help it or not, you are always the ultimate guarantor or destroyer of that innocence. And so, for a moment that night, all I could do was look up at the smiling little Obamas and pity them for everything they did not realize they were now going to lose: My heart broke, and I had this wild wish to undo everything we all had worked and hoped so hard, for so long, to bring about.

And then I noticed the way I seemed to be exempting myself, holding myself aloof, from responsibility for the kind of injury that I imagined Barack Obama had determined to inflict upon his children in the service of his conviction, his calling, his sense of duty, his altruism, his tragic or glorious destiny, and I felt the burden of my son weigh heavier on my own shoulders. You don't have to become the president of the United States to betray your children. Being a father is an unlimited obligation, one that even the best of us, with the least demanding of children, could never hope to fulfill entirely. Children's thirst for their fathers can never be slaked, no matter how bottomless and brimming the vessel. I have abandoned my children a thousand times, failed them, left their care and comfort to others, wandered in by telephone or e-mail from the void of a life on the road, issued arbitrary and contradictory commands from my mountaintop when all that was wanted was a place on my lap, absented myself from their bedtime routine on a night when they needed me more than usual, forestalled, deferred, or neglected their needs in the name of something I told myself merited the sacrifice. All that was in the very nature of fatherhood; it came with the territory.

Now, when I looked at Obama, whose own father had taken off when he was still a small boy, never to return, the pity I felt was for him. I hoisted my son higher on my shoulders and thought about his distant ancestor and namesake, armed with the fire and the knife of his great purpose, leading his son up Mount Moriah to pay the price that must be paid for the sacrifice that must be offered.

"Look at him," I urged my son. "Look at Barack. Look at Malia and Sasha. Abraham, look at them, remember them. You'll remember this night for the rest of your life."

"How do you know I won't forget?" my endlessly, implacably reasoning five-year-old said. He has always been a bit of a contrarian, and he may not have been fully in the spirit of Grant Park that night, either. "Maybe you won't *be* there."

He was right. I won't be there some day, one day, when he looks back and finds that he still remembers the faraway night on my long-departed shoulders, the night in Chicago when everything began to change, for him and for Malia and Sasha and for the world. But I didn't tell him that. Let him, let all of us, I thought, hold on to our innocence a little bit longer.

[III]

STRATEGIES FOR THE FOLDING OF TIME

To the Legoland Station

Squares and rectangles. That's what we had. Squares, rectangles, and wheels with chewy black rubber tires. Sloping red "roof" bricks of which there never seemed to be enough to cover a house. Trees shaped more like real trees than the schematic dendrites you get now. Windows and doors with snap-in glazing: more squares and rectangles. Six colors: basic red, white, blue, yellow, green, and black. And that was it.

Light blue, aquamarine, orange, purple, maroon, gold, silver, plum, pink—pink Legos!—and many shades of gray: Each of the original primary and secondary tones now has at least five variants, enabling the builder of, say, a Jawa Sandcrawler model to re-create the stippling of rust and corrosion in the Sandcrawler's hull by varying his palette of reds and grays. I still get a funny feeling, a kind of tiny spasm of moral revulsion, when I pick up a teal or lilac Lego. As for shape, Lego "bricks" left behind the orthogonal world years ago for a strange geometry of irregular polygons, a vast bestiary of hybrid pieces, custom pieces, blanks and inverts, clears and pearlescents, freaks that have their raised dots or their gripping tubes on more than one side at a time. And then there are the people—minifigs, as they're known among Legographers: Frankenstein monsters, American Indians, Jedi knights and pizza chefs, medieval crossbowmen and Vikings, deep-sea divers and bus drivers, Spider-Man, Harry Potter, Allen Iverson—the range of occupations and personalities to be found among the denizens of the Legosphere is so wide and elaborate that perhaps only the brain of an eight-year-old could possibly master it. I remember the sense of disdain I felt toward the cylinder-headed homunculi when minifigs began to be introduced, around the time when my original interest in Legos was waning. They didn't have the painted faces back then. Their heads were shiny yellow voids. Their arms and legs couldn't bend, and there was something of the nightmarish, something maimed, about them. But what I most resented about the minifigs was the scale they imposed on everything you built around them. Like Le Corbusier's humancentric Modulor scale or Leonardo's Vitruvian Man, the minifigs as they proliferated became the measure of all things: Weapons must fit their rigid grip, doorways accommodate the tops of their heads, cockpits accommodate their snap-on asses.

It was this sense of imposition, of predetermined boundaries and contours, of a formulary of play, that I found I most resented when Legos returned to my life, around the time my eldest child turned three. (She was into Indians, or rather, "Indians," especially Tiger Lily; we bought her a fairly complicated Lego set with war-painted minifigs, horses, tepees, a canoe, a rocky cliff.) But along with the giddy profusion of shapes and colors that had taken place during my long absence from the Legosphere, the underlying purpose of the toys also appeared to have changed.

When I first began to play with them in the late 1960s, Legos retained a strong flavor of their austere, progressive Scandinavian origins. Abstract, minimal, "pure" in form and design, they echoed the dominant midcentury aesthetic, with its emphasis on utility and human perfectibility. They were a lineal descendant of Friedrich Fröbel's famous "gifts," the wooden stacking blocks that influenced Frank Lloyd Wright as a child, part mathematics, part pedagogy, a system—the Lego System—by which children could be led to infer complex patterns from a few fundamental principles of interrelationship and geometry. They also made, and make to this day, a strong claim on a kid's senses, snapping together and coming apart with a satisfying dual appeal to the ear and the fingers. They presented the familiar objects one constructed with them—airplanes, houses, cars, faces—on a quirky grid, the world dissolved or simplified into big, chunky pixels.

In their limited repertoire of shapes and the absolute, even cruel, set of axioms governing the way they could and couldn't be arranged, Lego structures emphatically did not present—and in playing with them, you never hoped for—the appearance of reality. A Lego construction was not a scale model. It was an idealization, an approximation, your best version of the thing you were trying to make. Any house, any town, you built from Legos, with its airport and tramline and monorail, trim chimneys and grids of grass, automatically took on a certain social-democratic tidiness, even sterility (one of the notable qualities of acrylonitrile butadiene styrene, the material from which Lego bricks are made, is that it is sterile).

Orderly, functional, utopian, half imaginary, abstract, primary-colored—when I visited Helsinki a few years back, I felt as if I recognized it, the way you recognize a place from a dream.

By the late nineties, when my wife and I bought that first Indian set, abstraction was dead. Full-blown realism reigned supreme in the Legosphere. Legos were sold in kits that enabled one to put together—at fine scales, in detail made possible by a wild array of odd-shaped pieces—precise replicas of Ferrari Formula 1 racers, pirate galleons, jet airplanes. Lego provided not only the standard public-domain play environments supplied by toy designers of the past fifty to a hundred years—the Wild West, the Middle Ages, jungle and farm and city street—but also a line of licensed *Star Wars* kits, the first of many subsequent ventures into trademarked, conglomerate-owned, pre-imagined environments. Instead of the printed booklets I remembered, featuring suggestions for the kinds of things you might want to make from your box of squares and rectangles, the new kits came encumbered with fat, abstruse, wordless manuals that laid out, panel after numbered panel and page after page, the steps that must be followed if one hoped—and after all, why else would you nudge your dad into buying it for you?—to end up with a landspeeder just like Luke Skywalker's (only smaller). Where Lego-building had once been open-ended and exploratory, it now had far more in common with puzzle-solving, a process of moving incrementally toward an ideal, pre-established, and above all, a *provided* solution.

I resented this change. When my son and I finished putting together a TIE interceptor or Naboo starfighter, usually after several weeks of struggle, a half-deranged search for one tiny black chip of sterile styrene the size of his pinkie nail, and two or three bouts of prolonged despair, the resulting object was so undeniably handsome, and our investment of time in building it so immense, that the thought of playing with it, let alone ever disassembling it, was anathema. But more than the inherent difficulty—which, after all, is an important aspect of puzzle-solving, or the shift from exploration to reproduction—I resented the authoritarian nature of the new Lego. Though I admired and enjoyed *Toy Story* (1995), the film has always been tainted for me by its subtext of orthodoxy: its implied assertion that there is a right way and a wrong way to play with your toys. Andy, the young hero of *Toy Story*, uses his toys more or less the way their manufacturers intended—cowboys are cowboys; Mr. Potato Head, with his "angry eyes," is a suitable mustachioed villain—while the most telling sign that we are to take Sid, the quasi-psychotic neighbor kid, as a "bad boy" is that he hybridizes and "breaks the rules" of orderly play, equipping an Erector-set spider, for example, with a stubbly doll's head. Sid is mean, cruel, heartless, crazy: You can tell because he put his wrestler doll in a dress. A similar orthodoxy, a structure of control and implied obedience to the norms of the instruction manual and of the implacable exigencies of realism itself, seemed to have been unleashed, like the Dark Side of the Force, in the once bright Republic of Lego.

But I should have had more faith in my children, and in the saving power of the lawless imagination. Like all realisms, Lego realism was doomed. In part, this was an inevitable result of the quirks and limitations inherent in the Lego System, with the distortions that its various techniques of interlocking create. The addition of painted faces and elaborately modeled headgear, weapons, and accoutrements ultimately did little to diminish the fundamental silliness of the minifig; as with CGI animation, the technology falls down at the human form. In depicting people, it makes compromises that weaken the intended realism of the whole. But the technical limitations are only part of the greater failure of realism—defined as accuracy, precision, faithfulness to experience—to live up to the disorder, the unlikeliness, and the recombinant impulse of imagined experience.

Kids write their own manuals in a new language made up of the things we give them and the things that derive from the peculiar wiring of their heads. The power of Lego is revealed only after the models have been broken up or tossed, half finished, into the drawer. You sit down to make something and start digging around in the drawer or container, looking for a particular brick or axle, and the Legos circulate in the drawer with a peculiarly loud crunching noise. Sometimes you can't find the piece you're looking for, but a gear or a clear orange cone or a horned helmet catches your eye. Time after time, playing Legos with my kids, I would fall under the spell of the old familiar crunching. It's the sound of creativity itself, of the inventive mind at work, making something new out of what you have been given by your culture, what you know you will need to do the job, and what you happen to stumble on along the way.

All kids—the good ones, too—have a psycho tinge of Sid, of the maker of hybrids and freaks. My children have used aerodynamic, streamlined bits and pieces of a dozen *Star Wars* kits, mixed with Lego dinosaur jaws, Lego aqualungs, Lego doubloons, Lego tibias, to devise improbably beautiful spacecraft far more commensurate than George Lucas's with the mysteries of other galaxies and alien civilizations. They have equipped the manga-inspired Lego figures with Lego ichthyosaur flippers. When he was still a toddler, Abraham liked to put a glow-in-the-dark bedsheet-style Lego ghost costume over a Lego Green Goblin minifig and seat him on a Sioux horse, armed with a light saber, then make the Goblin do battle with a minifig Darth Vader, mounted on a black horse, armed with a bow and arrow. That is the aesthetic at work in the Legosphere now—not the modernist purity of the early years or the totalizing vision behind the dark empire of modern corporate marketing but the aesthetic of the Lego drawer, of the mash-up, the pastiche that destroys its sources at the same time that it makes use of and reinvents them. You churn around in the drawer and pull out what catches your eye, bits and pieces drawn from movies and history and your own fancy, and make something new, something no one has ever seen or imagined before.

The Wilderness of Childhood

When I was growing up, our house backed onto woods, a thin two-acre remnant of a once mighty Wilderness. This was in a Maryland city where the enlightened planners had provided a number of such lingering swaths of green. They were tame as can be, our woods, and yet at night they still filled with unfathomable shadows. In the winter they lay deep in snow and seemed to absorb, to swallow whole, all the ordinary noises of your body and your world. Scary things could still be imagined to take place in those woods. It was the place into which the bad boys fled after they egged your windows on Halloween and left your pumpkins pulped in the driveway. There were no Indians in those woods, but there had been once. We learned about them in school. Patuxent Indians, they'd been called. Swift, straight-shooting, silent as deer. Gone but for their lovely place names: Patapsco, Wicomico, Patuxent.

A minor but undeniable aura of romance was attached to the history of Maryland, my home state: refugee Catholic Englishmen, cavaliers in ringlets and ruffs; pirates, battles, the sack of Washington, "The Star-Spangled Banner," Harriet Tubman, Antietam. And when you went out into those woods behind our house, you could feel all that, all that history, those battles and dramas and romances, those stories. You could work it into your games, your imaginings, your lonely flights from the turmoil or torpor of your life at home. My friends and I spent hours there, braves, crusaders, commandos, blues and grays.

But the Wilderness of Childhood, as any kid could attest who grew up, like my father, on the streets of Flatbush in the forties, had nothing to do with trees or nature. I could lose myself on vacant lots and playgrounds, in the alleyway behind the Wawa, in the neighbors' yards, on the sidewalks. Anywhere, in short, I could reach on my bicycle, a 1970 Schwinn Typhoon, Coke-can red with a banana seat, a sissy bar, and ape-hanger handlebars. On it I covered the neighborhood in a regular route for half a mile in every direction. I knew the locations of all my classmates' houses, the number of pets and siblings they had, the brand of Popsicle they served, the potential dangerousness of their fathers. Matt Groening once did a great *Life in Hell* strip that took the form of a map of Bongo's neighborhood. At one end of a street that wound among yards and houses stood Bongo, the little one-eared rabbit boy. At the other stood his mother, about to blow her stack—Bongo was late for dinner again. Between Mother and Son lay the hazards— labeled ANGRY DOGS, ROVING GANG OF HOOLIGANS, GIRL WITH A CRUSH ON BONGO—of any journey through the Wilderness: deadly animals, antagonistic humans, lures and snares. It captured perfectly the mental maps of their worlds that children endlessly revise and refine. Childhood is a branch of cartography.

Most great stories of adventure, from *The Hobbit* to *Seven Pillars of Wisdom*, come furnished with a map. That's because every story of adventure is in part the story of a landscape, of the interrelationship between human beings (or Hobbits, as the case may be) and topography. Every adventure story is conceivable only in terms of the particular set of geographical features that in each case sets the course, literally, of the tale. But I think there is another, deeper reason for the reliable presence of maps in the pages, or on the endpapers, of an adventure story, whether that story is imaginatively or factually true. We have this idea of armchair traveling, of the reader who seeks in the pages of a ripping yarn or a memoir of polar exploration the kind of heroism and danger, in unknown, half-legendary lands, that he or she could never hope to find in life. This is a mistaken notion, in my view. People read stories of adventure—and write them—because they have themselves *been* adventurers. Childhood is, or has been, or ought to be, the great original adventure, a tale of privation, courage, constant vigilance, danger, and sometimes calamity. For the most part the young adventurer sets forth equipped only with the fragmentary map—marked HERE THERE BE TYGERS and MEAN KID WITH AIR RIFLE—that he or she has been able to construct out of a patchwork of personal misfortune, bedtime reading, and the accumulated local lore of the neighborhood children.

A striking feature of literature for children is the number of stories, many of them classics of the genre, that feature the adventures of a child, more often a group of children, acting in a world where adults, particularly parents, are completely or effectively out of the picture. Think of *The Lion, the Witch and the Wardrobe*, *The Railway Children*, or Charles Schulz's *Peanuts*. Philip Pullman's *His Dark Materials* trilogy presents a chilling version of this world in its depiction of Cittagazze, a city whose adults have all been stolen away. Then there is the very rich vein of children's literature featuring ordinary contemporary children navigating and adventuring through a contemporary, nonfantastical world that is nonetheless beyond the direct influence of adults, at least some of the time. I'm thinking the Encyclopedia Brown books, the Great Brain books, the Henry Reed and Homer Price books, the stories of the Mad Scientists' Club, a fair share of the early works of Beverly Cleary. As a kid, I was extremely fond of a series of biographies, largely fictional, I'm sure, that dramatized the lives of famous Americans—Washington, Jefferson, Kit Carson, Henry Ford, Thomas Edison, Daniel Boone—when they were children. (Boys, for the most part, though I do remember reading one about Clara Barton.) One element that was almost universal in these stories was the vast amounts of time the famous historical boys were alleged to have spent wandering with bosom companions, with friendly Indian boys or a devoted slave, through the once mighty wilderness, the Wilderness of Childhood, entirely free of adult supervision.

Though the wilderness available to me had shrunk to a mere green scrap of its former enormousness, though so much about childhood had changed in the years between the days of young George Washington's adventuring on his side of the Potomac and my own suburban exploits on mine, there was still a connected-ness there, a continuum of childhood. Eighteenth-century Virginia, twentieth-century Maryland, tenth-century Britain, Narnia, Neverland, Prydain—it was all the same Wilderness. Those legendary wanderings of Boone and Carson and young Daniel Beard (the father of the Boy Scouts of America), those games of war and exploration I read about, those frightening encounters with genuine menace, far from the help or interference of mother and father, seemed to me at the time—and I think this is my key point—absolutely familiar to me.

The thing that strikes me now when I think about the Wilderness of Childhood is the incredible degree of freedom my parents gave me to adventure there. A very grave, very significant shift in our idea of childhood has occurred since then. The Wilderness of Childhood is gone; the days of adventure are past. The land ruled by children, to which a kid might exile himself for at least some portion of every day from the neighboring kingdom of adulthood, has in large part been taken over, co-opted, colonized, and finally absorbed by the neighbors.

The traveler soon learns that the only way to come to know a city, to form a mental map of it, however provisional, and begin to find his or her own way around it, is to visit it alone, preferably on foot, and then become as lost as one possibly can. I have been to Chicago maybe a half-dozen times in my life, on book tours, and yet I still don't know my North Shore from my North Side, because every time I've visited, I have been picked up and driven around, and taken to see the sights by someone far more versed than I in the city's wonders and hazards. State Street, Halsted Street, the Loop—to me it's all a vast jumbled lot of stage sets and backdrops passing by the window of a car.

This is the kind of door-to-door, all-encompassing escort service that we adults have contrived to provide for our children. We schedule their encounters for them, driving them to and from one another's houses so they never get a chance to discover the unexplored lands between. If they are lucky, we send them out to play in the backyard, where they can be safely fenced in and even, in extreme cases, monitored with security cameras. When my family and I moved onto our street in Berkeley, the family next door included a nine-year-old girl; in the house two doors down the other way, there was a nine-year-old boy, her exact contemporary and, like her, a lifelong resident of the street. They had never met.

The sandlots and creek beds, the alleys and woodlands have been abandoned in favor of a system of reservations—Chuck E. Cheese, the Jungle, the Discovery Zone: jolly internment centers mapped and planned by adults with no blank spots aside from doors marked STAFF ONLY. When children roller-skate or ride their bikes, they go forth armored as for battle, and their parents typically stand nearby.

There are reasons for all of this. The helmeting and monitoring, the corralling of children into certified zones of safety, is in part the product of the *Consumer Reports* mentality, the generally increased consciousness, in America, of safety and danger. To this one might add the growing demands of insurance actuarials and the national pastime of torts. But the primary reason for this curtailing of adventure, this closing off of Wilderness, is the increased anxiety we all feel over the abduction of children by strangers; we fear the wolves in the Wilderness. This is not a rational fear; in 1999, for example, according to the Justice Department, the number of stranger abductions in the United States was 115. Such crimes have always occurred at about the same rate; being a child is exactly no more and no less dangerous than it ever was. What has changed is that the horror is so much better known. At times it seems as if parents are being deliberately encouraged to fear for their children's lives, though only a cynic would suggest there was money to be made in doing so.

The endangerment of children—that persistent theme of our lives, arts, and literature over the past twenty years—resonates so strongly because, as parents, as members of preceding generations, we look at the poisoned legacy of modern industrial society and its ills, at the world of strife and radioactivity, climatological disaster, overpopulation, and commodification, and feel guilty. As the national feeling of guilt over the extermination of the Indians led to the creation of a kind of cult of the Indian, so our children have become cult objects to us, too precious to be risked. At the same time they have become fetishes, the objects of an unhealthy and diseased fixation. And once something is fetishized, capitalism steps in and finds a way to sell it.

What is the impact of the closing down of the Wilderness on the development of children's imaginations? This is what I worry about the most. I grew up with a freedom, a liberty that now seems breathtaking and almost impossible. Recently, my younger daughter, after the usual struggle and exhilaration, learned to ride her bicycle. Her joy at her achievement was rapidly followed by a creeping sense of puzzlement and disappointment as it became clear to both of us that there was nowhere for her to ride it—nowhere that I was willing to let her go. Should I send my children out to play? There is a small grocery store around the corner, not over two hundred yards from our front door. Can I let her ride there alone to experience the singular pleasure of buying herself an ice cream on a hot summer day and eating it on the sidewalk, alone with her thoughts? Soon after she learned to ride, we went out together after dinner, she on her bike, with me following along at a safe distance behind. What struck me at once on that lovely summer evening, as we wandered the streets of our lovely residential neighborhood at that after-dinner hour that had once represented the peak moment, the magic hour of my own childhood, was that we didn't encounter a single other child.

Even if I do send them out, will there be anyone to play with?

Art is a form of exploration, of sailing off into the unknown alone, heading for those unmarked places on the map. If children are not permitted—not taught—to be adventurers and explorers as children, what will become of the world of adventure, of stories, of literature itself?

Hypocritical Theory

I hate Captain Underpants.

I'm not saying that the books in the popular series, featuring the adventures of two potty-minded fourth-graders, written and illustrated by Dav Pilkey, aren't lively, well crafted, and snappily designed. Nor am I saying that the books' unrelenting, quasi-Tourettic aesthetic of poop, boogers, and toilets isn't rooted in an authentic moment of childhood—of boyhood, at any rate. I'm just saying that I hate them. I feel obliged to hate them, even though hating them makes me a hypocrite. I'm a father. Being a hypocrite is my job.

Proof of my hypocrisy can be found in my ancient devotion to the drugstore cult of Wacky Packages. Wacky Packages followed Hot Wheels and preceded Pet Rocks as one of the great commercial fads of my childhood. For about a year, like all my friends, I collected Wacky Packages, traded them, stuck them to my three-ring binder, the inside of my locker, my bedroom wastebasket. They were so popular and ubiquitous that Topps Chewing Gum,

Inc., the manufacturer of Wacky Packages, several times literally ran out of paper to print them on. Just before the fad petered out, Wacky Packages were featured on the cover of *New York* magazine (my parents had a subscription), which used the fad to diagnose me and my supposedly cynical, wised-up, skeptical generation.

The typical Wacky Packages card featured a peel-off sticker that mocked the appearance and name of some well-known brand of household product, grocery item, or staple of the drugstore. A bottle of fetid-looking salad dressing labeled Fish-Bone, a foam-mouthed dog on the label of a can of Rabid Shave shaving cream, a Bustedfinger candy bar with a big swollen finger poking through the wrapper, a bar of Vile soap. A checklist card came in every package, along with a square of chewable pink cellulose, and every few months Topps would bring out a new series. Topps card designer Art Spiegelman and his colleagues (among them the great pulp-magazine cover artist Norman Saunders and underground-comix stalwarts Kim Deitch, Bill Griffith, Jay Lynch, and Bhob Stewart) wound the spiral of mockery so tight that the fourth series featured a card depicting Wormy Packages, worm-infested trading stickers intended (like Wacky Packages themselves, like all the products and advertisements they mocked, like everything, by implication, that you saw, heard, or paid attention to, every moment of your young media-saturated life) to pry loose a nickel from your pocket.

To any kid who had picked up a copy of *Mad* magazine during the previous twenty years, there was nothing new or generationally distinctive about the flavor of mockery to which Wacky Packages subjected the features of the American brandscape.

The salient novelty of Wacky Packages was not their irreverence toward copywriter clichés or subversion of the ineluctability of brands and logos but their free, and at the time, startling use of "gross" humor. The first few series of cards employed imagery such as lice, poisonous dog food, exposed brains, Putrid cat chow, maggots, toe corns, flesh peeled away by Band-Ache strips, a powdered-blood breakfast drink for vampires (Fang), and saliva. What made that kind of imagery so startling was not the humor itself. Gross or sick humor was a fundamental mode of children's discourse. Dead-baby jokes; songs about vomit, snot, diarrhea, and other forms of excrement; anecdotes and urban legends of cannibalism, coprophagia, brain-eating earwigs—at the age of eight or nine, along with all of my peers, I had assumed custody of a vast repertoire of wondrously disgusting material. The shock value of Wacky Packages had nothing to do with, in this sense, their content. They depicted or referred to nothing that I had not imagined, rhymed about, discussed, drawn, or seen for myself. What was so shocking about Wacky Packages was that they were a production of the adult world. Adults had conceived and painted them; adults had manned the rotating drums of the printing presses and the machine that wrapped each pack of two cards in waxed paper; adults had trucked the Wacky Packages to the drugstore, where you handed over your five cents to an adult who, perhaps most shockingly of all, allowed you to buy them. It was as if your mother encouraged you to play with your food, or your father handed you his expensive German shortwave radio and a screwdriver and told you to go right ahead and figure out how the damn thing worked.

In retrospect, I see the early-1973 Wacky Packages craze as a pivotal moment in the history of American childhood. Prior to this, gross humor was a kind of code, a thieves' argot spoken only when out of earshot of adults, who—one knew it on faith if not through painful experience—never would have permitted or approved of it. Would not have understood it, in fact. Songs about boogers and vomit were transmissions in a frequency that would sound to the adult ear like infuriating squawk, annoying static. And that was their point. Along with the unwritten rules and nuances of byzantine games played in vacant lots and alleyways, gross humor was a principal means by which children signaled and celebrated the absence of adults in the immediate vicinity. We were a generation—maybe the last full generation—that adults left alone, at least sometimes. Singing a disgusting song or telling a cruel riddle (Q: What do you call a man with no arms or legs when you throw him in the ocean? A: Bob) was like running up an insurgent flag in a neighborhood where the occupier had been driven back for the moment. At the same time, the gore and mayhem, the amputations, the fatalities, the abominations described by gross humor also constituted a way of acknowledging the implicit danger of living in a world devoid of adults and of the protection they theoretically afforded.

The adults who sold us Wacky Packages spoke the secret language; they entered boldly into the preserve or magic ghetto of childhood under the insurgent flag. I remember how it felt to open those first packs of Wacky Packages stickers: delicious, incredible, pleasurable in the way that only something truly wrong can be.

Because in the long run, Wacky Packages, and the cultural trend of which they turned out to be the leading edge, were bad for children. I don't mean bad in any kind of easy, moralistic way. Children must learn to mock capitalism and the uses to which it seeks to put them as early as they learn how to swim. And I wouldn't care—I'd secretly applaud it—if my son and his friends wasted every free moment they had creating taxonomies of vomit by chunkiness and color. It's just that they now have so few moments that can be said to be free in any sense of the word. So much of their culture—that compound of lore and play—is now the trademarked product and property of adults. The men who sold us Wacky Packages were like those traders in Hudson's Bay blankets—good, warm blankets—whose stock gradually drove out the native product and sent the traditional weaving craft into decline. We sold out our liberty and gave up control over our ancient heritage of vulgarity for the thrill of seeing it done up in four-color lithography, transferable to a notebook or a classroom desk, scented with the sweet dust of bubble gum.

After Wacky Packages came Slime, the first "disgusting" toy (1977), and Garbage Pail Kids stickers (1985) and the advent of fart jokes in Walt Disney cartoons (*The Lion King*, 1994) and that masterpiece of the confectioner's art, Sour Flush, acrid sweet powder that comes packaged in a miniature plastic toilet to be dabbed at and consumed by means of the moistened end of an edible plunger. And then one day children looked around and saw that there was no corner, no alleyway, no space anywhere in their lives that was free of adult supervision, adult mediation, adult control. All sports are organized sports, trick-or-treating takes place in school gymnasiums, and parents who send their children out to play where I used to play, in the street—in the street!—court well-publicized tragedies such as abduction and intervention by the minions of Child Protective Services. Captain Underpants, champion of flatulence and bodily fluids, is a mainstay of the Scholastic Book Club. The reading of the books is not only condoned but encouraged by teachers and librarians, grateful that boys are interested in reading anything at all.

In detesting, disapproving of the Captain Underpants books, I am not trying to disparage my son's taste in fiction, to belittle his choices, to withhold my approval of him. God knows I have nothing against boogers. This is where the hypocrisy comes in. I loved Wacky Packages. I knew every foul verse of the classic anthems "Suffocation" (Suffocation, mental retardation / Suffocation, the game we like to play) and "Diarrhea" (later made famous in the film *Parenthood*). If Captain Underpants had been around when I was a kid, I probably would have loved him, too. But knowing that doesn't make it any harder for me to wish Captain Underpants away. The irony of the series is too painful. George and Harold, the young protagonists, enjoy the unscheduled time and freedom from adult supervision that I (and no doubt Dav Pilkey) once took for granted. The boys imagine, create, and draw their own superhero adventures (including those of Super Diaper Baby) within the context of an old-fashioned adult world that still disapproves heartily of boys' taking pleasure from talking about pee and poop and snot. George and Harold's teachers, one comes to realize, would never allow them to read Captain Underpants books, let alone help win free copies of them for their classroom by placing book-club orders with Scholastic. The original spirit of mockery has been completely inverted; it is now the adult world that mocks children, implicitly and profitably, speaking its old language, invoking its bygone secret pleasures.

I see my disapproval of Captain Underpants, therefore, as a drawing of a line between my son and me, between his world and mine, between adulthood and childhood, as a small, feeble attempt to reestablish the contours of a boundary that in the greater culture has grown vague, disregarded, abused. If I withdraw my approval of Captain Underpants—if I tell my son I will gladly supply him with good books and comics but that if he wants to read those damned Captain Underpants, he'll have to pay for them himself—that withdrawal creates a gap, a small enchanted precinct of parental disapproval within which he can curl up, for a minute, for the time it takes to read a crass, vibrant, silly 120-page book with big print, one that he paid for himself, and thrill to the deep, furtive pleasure of annoying one's father. There is no way to draw that line, to re-create that boundary, without engaging in hypocrisy, without condemning, questioning, or diminishing the importance of the things, from ultra-sugary bubble gum to trans-fatty snacks to Humboldt County sinsemilla, that once stood at the center of my way of loving the world. That's what sucks about being an adult. Adulthood has always carried a burden of self-denial, of surrendering pleasures, of leaving childish things behind. Maybe that's why, around thirty years ago, adults started trying to get out of the adult business and into the business of selling childhood. Or maybe it's that self-denial, surrender, and forswearing are a lot harder to package for retail. It could be hypocrisy is such a toxin that our society is better off without it, even if that means infantilizing adults with late-night programming on the Cartoon Network or merchandising children's once autonomous culture back to them in shrink-wrapped packs. But it's hard to think of anything that would be more hypocritical than the selling, to children whose lives we control and regiment down to the quarter hour, of brightly colored confectionery visions of children who are still subject to creative neglect, still free to engage in the most profitable of human activities: wasting time making up crass, vibrant silliness that is all your own.

The Splendors of Crap

A t least once a month I take my kids to see a new "family movie"—the latest computer-generated piece of animated crap. Please don't oblige me to revisit the last one even long enough to name the film, let alone describe it. Anyway, you know the one I mean: set in a zoo, or in a forest, or on a farm, or under the sea, or in "Africa," or in an effortfully hilarious StorybookLand™ where magic, wonder, and make-believe are ironized and mocked except at those moments when they are tenderly invoked to move units. I believe but am not prepared to swear that the lead in this weekend's version may have been a neurotic lion, or a neurotic bear, or a neurotic rat, or a neurotic chicken. Chances are good that the thing featured penguins; for a while the movies have all been featuring penguins. Naturally, there were the legally required 5.5 incidences of humor-simulating flatulence per hour of running time. A raft of bright pop-punk tunes on the sound track, alternating with familiar numbers culled with art and cruelty from the storehouse of parental nostalgia. Creativity, idiosyncrasy, and the fertile rebelliousness of a romantic dreamer were invoked and glorified without recourse to the use or display of any of those three unmarketable commodities.

In principle and in many instances, both as a parent and as a former child, I have nothing against crappy art and the ancillary crap—the extruded action figures and rubber-transfer-stiffened underpants and books of unpeelable stickers, sold separately—that inevitably attends it. First of all, what smells strongly of crap to one generation—Victorian penny dreadfuls, the music of the Archies, the Lone Ranger radio show, blaxploitation films of the seventies—so often becomes a fruitful source of inspiration, veneration, and study for those to come, while certified Great and Worthy Art molders and fades on its storage rack, giving off an increasingly powerful whiff of naphthalene.

More central to my regard—in principle, at least—for the artistic possibilities of crap is my lifelong personal experience with the power of mass art to transport and enrich the imagination of its consumer. I saw a lot of lousy movies and watched a ton of crappy television and read a bunch of utterly forgettable books and comics and listened to hours of junk music as a kid. And I'm still drawing profitably in my own art on some of the tawdry treasure I stored up in those years.

But the acceptance and even the glorification of crap implies no universal obligation. Even without the benefit of generational hindsight, there are distinctions to be made among varieties of crap, and to that end I find myself thinking back to a Saturday afternoon thirty years ago when I went over to the Megginsons' house to play *Planet of the Apes.*

There were four Megginson children: Peter, Caroline, Andrew, and Jane. Caroline and I were classmates and Peter, a year older, was my best friend. They lived with their mother in a modest three-bedroom town house at the other end of the Village of Long Reach, in Columbia, Maryland, my hometown. Peter and Caroline each had a room, and the younger pair shared; Mrs. Megginson slept, not without a certain mysteriousness, in a semi-secret basement lair. She was a calligrapher, and the house was filled with the wise sentiments of the revered minds of the day rendered in Mrs. Megginson's handsome hand. My parents kept a tidy house, but Mrs. Megginson's laxity as a housekeeper was a point of pride with her, and visitors were cheerfully advised to wash the roach shit from cups and plates taken from her kitchen cabinets. The Megginson father was missing and rarely mentioned, the family budget extremely tight, the car an orange two-stroke Beetle named Agnes (it said so in adhesive calligraphy on her doors). There was always a faint air of possible trouble in the air, a sense that Mrs. Megginson, in her ongoing, hitherto successful efforts to raise four good children on her own, was operating just outside the bounds of accepted suburban-Maryland practice, with financial calamity a real if not quite imminent possibility. I suppose, looking back, that the Megginsons lived nearly as much in bohemia as in Columbia, and these were my first visits to that precarious kingdom.

Through some alchemy of the mother's artistic nature, the openness of the household, the unfettered nature of American childhood during that time and the sheer mass of children in the house, there was always something afoot at the Megginsons'. When you walked in the door, you would get drafted into whatever large ongoing collective enterprise was under way—making that year's Halloween costumes, re-creating in card stock and glue a shot of Camelot from a panel in *Prince Valiant*, writing a rock opera, helping to cope through pie, sauce, and butter with a rapidly spoiling surfeit of apples gathered at Sewell's Orchard. Usually, some book, TV show, or record album was passionately in vogue around the house, with all play activity—drawing sessions, outdoor adventuring, dinner-table confabulation—focused narrowly around *Norse Gods and Giants* or *Space: 1999* or *Queen II*. And like one of the progressive rock bands then in their heyday, the Megginsons were busy, all the time, not only with those big double-sided concept albums but with all manner of side projects and solo albums and one-shots: Caroline was learning to read Tarot cards; Peter had found a way to make cool-looking spaceships out of the cap from a Bic pen and the plastic clip from a bread bag snapped in two; Andrew was immersed in the epistemology of Tintin; Jane could not stop talking about Ginnungagap.

On this one Saturday morning, the Megginsons were all about *Planet of the Apes*. Not the movie nor any of its five increasingly baroque sequels, and certainly not the Pierre Boulle novel, confusingly replete with witty Frenchmen. No, the Megginsons and I were obsessed with the short-lived CBS television series, of which thirteen episodes aired, to low ratings, at the end of 1974.

As with many forgotten TV series, all the episodes of *Planet of* the Apes are now available on DVD, but I haven't ever gone back to look at them. What I remember about the show, albeit vaguely, are the elements that formed the basis of our play: the setting amid a world of forests and grassy hills; the peculiarity that, unlike in the films, the humans, though degraded in ape eyes, were capable of speech; and above all, perhaps, the steady presence in every episode of adventure on horseback.

For a day we inhabited our Planet of the Apes: a hill, a stream, a small wooden bridge behind the Megginsons' disorderly and productive town house at the ragged edge of Columbia, where built land gave way to open space. According to principles implied but never articulated by the TV show, we named and fitted ourselves with weapons and histories. I can't quite remember who was a sensitive chimpanzee, who a questing astronaut, who a noble savage, who a brutal and potent gorilla warlord, but I know that nobody wanted to be one of the characters from the show. It was always part of the game to make up your own character. Maybe we all wanted to be astronauts and left the marauding and enslaving gorillas to be played by the heavies of our imaginations. I am sure that at least as much time was spent in preparing to play, in conferring and arguing and revising the parameters of the game, as in actually playing it. Eventually, night fell; it was time to come inside, time for me to return to my own neater, more secure, vastly emptier house.

And now I have four children of my own, two girls and two boys. There is a lot going on in my house, and sometimes it seems to echo or reflect the fertile chaos in the Megginsons'. But somehow it is not quite the same. I'm not sure what the reason for that is. We don't let things get as messy around here. My kids have a lot more homework than I ever did. But there's something lacking in their lives, and I see it in their relation to the variety of crap that now dominates the mass-art landscape, a variety well represented by neurotic-farting-penguin movies.

There's no doubt that the *Planet of the Apes* TV show was crap. Yes, the makeup was decent for its time, and the shows tried, in the dutiful manner of early seventies post–*Star Trek*, pre–*Star Wars* television science fiction, to address weighty issues of prejudice, intolerance, and the meaning of being human. But it remained— indeed its existence depended on it being—a knockoff of a knock- off, the sequel to sequels, worked up by veteran TV hacks to fill up the spaces between Parkay margarine ads. What's more, it was crap that flopped, canceled after only three months.

But it had—crucially, to my theory of what makes great mass art—the powerful quality of being open-ended, vague at its bor- ders. Onto its simple template of horses and apes and humans, of quest and pursuit across a simplified landscape, a kid could easily project himself and the world he lived in. In its very incomplete- ness, born of lack of budget, the loose picaresque structure, and even of cancellation itself, it hinted at things beyond its own bor- ders. There was room for you and your imagination in the narra- tive map of the show.

The CGI animated movies that dominate in the theaters today don't work that way. With their fixed sets of characters, each gi- raffe or squirrel resembling in its carefully designed variation not a recognizable person or type so much as a brand identity, these films operate more like classic sitcoms than like the parodic-adventure stories for which they try to pass. The contours of the worlds they depict feel as backless as painted scenery flats, as the walls and doors of Mary Richards's newsroom or the Huxtable living room. I like a good sitcom as much as anybody, but did any kids ever try to get up a game of *Murphy Brown*? At the same time, the ample budgets, large crews, and generally high level of technical prowess boasted by even the most execrable of these films enable their creators to employ the prevailing *Star Wars*–inspired aesthetic of packing every scene, every frame, with incident and filigree, without the concomitant open-ended structure that made the early *Star Wars* films, at least, a likely locus of fantasy play both for children and, in the form of fan fiction, adults. The new studio-made CGI products are like unctuous butlers of the imagination, ready to serve every need or desire as it arises; they don't leave anything implied, unstated, incomplete. There is no room in them for children. And so they never form the basis for my own kids' games.

As a father raised on a hearty diet of crap, I wrestle all the time with the role of crap in my own kids' lives. There is so damn much of it now—crap TV shows, crap movies, crap toys and crap trading cards, crap video games, crap Flash animations and crap macaroni and cheese with SpongeBob-shaped pasta nodules, all of it interlocked and cross-referenced with breathtaking care and thoroughness. But I wouldn't worry about it so much, I guess, if I felt like my kids had the space in their own heads and, especially, in their own physical worlds to lay it all out and make it their own.

Sometimes they don't seem able to operate in an imaginative world. When we go to Maine in the summer my wife and I open the back door and step aside and wait for them to fly out into the grass and the sunshine. Acres of woods and wildflowers, butterflies and streams, a tame waterfall. A waterfall and hours of freedom from rules and parental control. And they stand there on the doorstep, eyeing one another, shuffling from foot to foot.

In *The Omnivore's Dilemma* Michael Pollan describes the disillusioning reality of the life of chickens sold as "free-range." He explains that these birds are raised, like all commercially farmed chicken, in the dense confinement of industrial henhouses for the first six weeks of their lives. At the end of that period, not long before the chickens are to be slaughtered, the doors of the henhouse are rolled open, giving onto a regulation patch of open range. The chickens come to the door and look out at the world of green grass and grubworms and fresh air they are being offered. And then they go back to the cramped, safe remainder of their lives, with their needs and desires attended to as assiduously as by any butler or animation studio. They are afraid to go outside; it's not a world they know or know how to explore. The farmers don't really want them to go out and explore it; there are too many diseases they might catch, unprotected by antibiotics as they are.

My kids are free-range children, in all the stark reality of the term except the part about being eaten. If, like the four Pevensie children (two boys and two girls) of *The Lion, the Witch and the Wardrobe*, they were sent off to the countryside to avoid the Blitz, my children might well have to be marched, under protest, to the room with the old wardrobe and shoved in among the coats; it would be hard for them to grasp how an entire old house, filled with unknown rooms and corridors, might become a world of unlimited play. They might never be able to engage in the half-bored, half-enchanted wandering through the variable, never-changing spectacle of the neighborhood that enables the children (three boys and a girl) in Edward Eager's *Half Magic* to find the talisman that grants half of every wish, so that one must learn, invaluably, to wish twice as hard.

That may be why I spend as much time worrying about the crap in my kids' imaginative diet as I do fretting over their eating habits. Free space, free play, and the sense of independent control over a world that is vague and discoverable at its edges: These act as a kind of filtration system enabling kids not to work the crap out of their minds—I proclaim for all time the splendor and goodness of crap entertainment—but to compound it with the alloy of their own imagination, tempering it against the hard edges and rough spots of the physical world. All great crap is open-ended but only if it can be carried by a child right out into the open. Otherwise, kids get trapped within the flats of the vivid and convincing set that we have constructed for them, afraid to go through doors that lead nowhere, staring through a CGI window at a pastel-and-pixel view of a world they fear or have forgotten how to reach.

EXERCISES IN MASCULINE AFFECTION

The Hand on My Shoulder

didn't play golf, and he had never smoked marijuana. I was a nail chewer, inclined to brood, and dubious of the motives of other people. He was big and placid, uniformly kind to strangers and friends, and never went anywhere without whistling a little song. I minored in philosophy. He fell asleep watching television. He fell asleep in movie theaters, too, and occasionally, I suspected, while driving. He had been in the navy during World War II, which taught him, he said, to sleep whenever he could. I, still troubled no doubt by perplexing questions of ontology and epistemology raised during my brief flirtation with logical positivism ten years earlier, was an insomniac. I was also a Jew, of a sort; he was, when required, an Episcopalian.

He was not a big man, but his voice boomed, and his hands were meaty, and in repose there was something august about his heavy midwestern features: pale blue eyes that, in the absence of hopefulness, might have looked severe; prominent, straight nose and heavy jowls that, in the absence of mirth, might have seemed imperious and disapproving. Mirth and hopefulness, however, were never absent from his face. Some people, one imagines, may be naturally dauntless and buoyant of heart, but with him, good spirits always seemed, far more admirably, to be the product of a strict program of self-improvement in his youth—he believed, like most truly modest men, in the absolute virtue of self-improvement— which had wrought deep, essential changes in a nature inclined by birth to the darker view and gloominess that cropped up elsewhere in the family tree. He didn't seem to be happy out of some secret knowledge of the essential goodness of the world, or from having fought his way through grief and adversity to a hard-won sense of his place in it; they were simple qualities, his good humor and his optimism, unexamined, automatic, stubborn. I never failed to take comfort in his presence.

The meaning of divorce will elude us as long as we are blind to the meaning of marriage, as I think at the start we must all be. Marriage seems—at least it seemed to an absurdly young man in the summer of 1987, standing on the sun-drenched patio of an elegant house on Lake Washington—to be an activity, like chess or tennis or a rumba contest, that we embark upon in tandem while everyone who loves us stands around and hopes for the best. We have no inkling of the fervor of their hope, nor of the ways in which our marriage, that collective endeavor, will be constructed from and burdened with their love.

When I look back—always an unreliable procedure, I know—it seems to have been a case of love at first sight. I met him, his wife, and their yellow beach house all on the same day. It was a square-

pillared bungalow, clapboard and shake, the color of yellow gingham, with a steep pitched roof and a porch that looked out over
a frigid but tranquil bay of brackish water. His wife, like him in
the last years of a vigorous middle age, had been coming to this
stretch of beach since early in her girlhood, and for both her and
her daughter, whom I was shortly to marry, it was more heavily
and richly layered with memories, associations, artifacts, and stories than any place any member of my own family had lived since
we had left Europe seventy years before. Everything about this
family was like that. My future mother-in-law lived in the house
in Seattle where she had been born. My father-in-law had grown
up down the road in Portland. They had met at the University of
Washington. Everyone they knew, they had known for longer than
I'd been alive. All the restaurants they favored had been in business for years, they were charter members of their country club,
and in some cases they did business with the sons of tradesmen
they had dealt with in the early days of their marriage. A journey
through the drawers, closets, and cabinets of their house in town
yielded a virtual commercial and social history of Seattle, in the
form of old matchboxes, rulers, pens, memo pads, napkins, shot
glasses, candy tins, golf tees, coat hangers; years and years' worth
of lagniappes, giveaways, souvenirs, and mementos bearing the
names, in typefaces of four decades, of plumbing supply companies, fuel oil dealers, newlyweds, dry cleaners, men and women
celebrating birthdays and anniversaries.

God, it was a seductive thing to a deracinated, assimilated,
uncertain, wandering young Jew whose own parents had not been

married for years and no longer lived anywhere near the house in Maryland where, for want of a truer candidate, he had more or less grown up. They were in many ways classic WASPs, to be sure, golfing, khaki-wearing, gin-drinking WASPs. The appeal of such people and their kind of world to a young man such as I was has been well-documented in film and literature; perhaps enough to seem by now a bit outdated. But it wasn't, finally, a matter of class or style, though they had both. I fell in love with their rooted-ness, with the visible and palpable continuity of their history as a family in Seattle, with their ability to bring a box of photographs taken thirty summers earlier and show me the room I was sitting in before it was painted white, the madrone trees that screened the porch before two fell over, the woman I was going to marry digging for geoduck clams on the beach where she had just lain sunbathing.

Of course, they were more than a kind of attractive gift wrap for their photographs, houses, and the historical contents of their drawers. They were ordinary, problematical people, my in-laws, forty years into a complicated marriage, and over the course of my own brief marriage to their daughter, I came to love and appreci-ate them both as individuals, on their merits and, as my marriage began so quickly to sour, for the endurance of their partnership. They had that blind, towering doggedness of the World War II generation. I suppose it's possible that with two daughters, they'd always wanted a son, my father-in-law especially; I do know for certain that I have never been one to refuse the opportunity to add another father to my collection.

He offered himself completely, without reservation, though in his own particular, not to say limited, way (it is this inherent limited quality of fathers and their love that motivates collectors like me to try to amass a complete set). He took me down to Nordstrom, the original store in downtown Seattle, and introduced me to the man who sold him his suits. I bought myself a few good square-cut, sober-colored numbers in a style that would not have drawn a second glance on Yesler Way in 1954. He introduced me to the woman from whom he bought jewelry for his wife, to the man who took care of his car, to all of the golf buddies and cronies whose sons he had been admiring from afar for the last thirty years. He was a bit barrel-chested anyway, but whenever we went anywhere together and, as was all but inevitable, ran into someone he knew, his breast, introducing me, seemed to grow an inch broader, the hand on my shoulder would administer a little fight-trainer massage, and I would feel him—as first the wedding and, later, the putative grandchildren drew nearer—placing, for that moment, all his hopes in me. He took me to football games, basketball games, baseball games. He let me drive his Cadillac; naturally, he never drove anything else. Most of all, however—most important to both of us—he let me hang out in his den.

As the child of divorced parents, myself divorced, and a writer trained by five hundred years of European and American literary history always to search out the worm in the bud, I have, of necessity, become a close observer of other people's marriages. I have noticed that in nearly all the longest-lived ones, if there is space enough in the house, each partner will have a room to flee to. If, however, there is only one room to spare, it will always be the husband's. My in-laws had plenty of room, but while she had her office just off the bedroom (where I would sometimes see her sitting at a Chinese desk, writing a letter or searching for an article clipped from *Town & Country* about flavoring ice creams with edible flowers), my mother-in-law's appeared to serve a largely ceremonial function.

My father-in-law, on the other hand, sometimes seemed to live down in the basement. His office, like him, was mostly about golf. The carpet was Bermuda-grass green, the walls were hung with maps of St. Andrews and framed *New Yorker* covers of duffers, and the various hats, ashtrays, hassocks, cigarette lighters, plaques, novelty telephones, and trophies around the room were shaped like golf balls, tees, mashies, mulligans, and I don't know what. In the midst of all this sat an enormous black Robber Baron desk with matching black Captain Nemo chair; an old, vaguely Japanese-looking coffee table on its last tour of duty in the house; a cyclopean television; and a reclining armchair and sofa, both covered in wool patterned with the tartan of some unknown but no doubt staunch, whiskey-drinking, golf-wild highland clan.

It is for just such circumstances, in which two men with little in common may find themselves thrown together with no other recourse than to make friends, that sports were invented. When my wife and I visited I went downstairs, flopped on the sofa, and watched a game with my father-in-law. He made himself a C.C. and soda, and sometimes, to complete the picture, I let him mix one for me. Like many men of my generation, I found solace when unhappy in placing quotation marks around myself and everything I did. There was I, an "unhappy husband," drinking a "cocktail" and "watching the game." This was the only room in the house where I was permitted to smoke—I have long since quit—and I made the most of it (a man's den often serves the same desublimating function in the household as Mardi Gras or Las Vegas in the world; a different law obtains there). We spent hours together, cheering on Art Monk and Carlton Fisk and other men whose names, when by chance they arise now, can summon up that entire era of whiskey and football and the smell of new Coupe de Ville, when the biggest mistake I ever made came home to roost, and I briefly had one of the best fathers I've ever found.

My ex-wife and I—I won't go into the details—had good times and bad times, fought and were silent, tried and gave up and tried some more before finally throwing in the towel, focused, with the special self-absorption of the miserable, on our minute drama and its reverberations in our own chests. All the while, the people who loved us were not sitting there whispering behind their hands like spectators at a chess match. They were putting our photographs in frames on their walls. They were uniting our names over and over on the outsides of envelopes that bore anniversary wishes and recipes clipped from newspapers. They were putting our birthdays in their address books, knitting us socks, studying the fluctuating fortunes of our own favorite hitters every morning in the box scores. They were working us into the fabric of their lives. When at last we broke all those promises that we thought we had made only to each other, in an act of faithlessness whose mutuality appeared somehow to make it all right, we tore that fabric, not irrecoverably but deeply. We had no idea how quickly two families can work to weave themselves together. When I saw him sometime later at his mother's funeral in Portland, my father-in-law told me that the day my divorce from his daughter came through was the saddest one in his life. Maybe that was when I started to understand what had happened.

What was I now to him? How can it have felt to have been divorced by someone he treated like a son? These are not considerations that comfort me or make me especially proud. I try to remind myself that in the long course of his life, I occupied only a tiny span of years toward the end, when everything gleams with an unconvincing luster, moving too quickly to be real. And I try to forget that for a short while I formed a layer, however thin, in the deep stratigraphy of his family, so that some later explorer, rummaging through the drawers of his big old desk, might brush aside a scorecard from the 1967 PGA Pacific Northwest Open signed by Arnold Palmer, or an old pencil-style typewriter eraser with a stiff brush on one end, stamped QUEEN CITY RIBBON CO., and turn up a faded photograph of me, in my sober blue suit, flower in my lapel, looking as if I knew what I was doing.

The Story of Our Story

'm reading *The Arabian Nights*, in Husain Haddawy's wonderful translation, and I'm struck by the presence in the book's frame story—surely the single most beautiful story any human being has ever told—of a girl named Dinarzad. Everyone remembers the older sister, Shahrazad, wily and noble, who saves her own life and the life of all the maidens in the kingdom by spinning out a thousand and one nocturnal stories to the wife-murdering king Shahriyar; but no one ever seems to recall the nightly attendance, in that fraught bedroom, of young Dinarzad, even though her presence is crucial to the working out of Shahrazad's plan. For the job entrusted to Dinarzad is the universal job of younger siblings the world over: not merely to witness history but to demand it. It is Dinarzad night after night—not the king—who speaks up, asking (as Haddawy renders it), "Please, sister, if you are not sleepy, tell us one of your little tales to while away the night." Shahrazad's sister thrives—survives—on her sister's stories and recollections of stories, and by gently demanding them, she ensures the salvation of herself and her elder sibling, whom she obliges, in so demanding, to become a hero.

My younger brother's wife came home from the hospital yesterday with their second child, another boy, and this new pair of brothers has me thinking about the boys' father and me. Our mother brought Steve home laid across a hospital blanket, asleep on his belly, red-faced and milky-eyed, no longer than the width of her lap. I'd been waiting for him on the patio of the apartment, and when the family car, a white Dodge Coronet 550, finally pulled into our assigned spot, I shuffled half unwilling down the grassy knoll to the parking lot to get my first long look at him. I had been alive for five years, three months, and fifteen days. In that time I had known love and sorrow. I had lived in Silver Spring, Staten Island, Pittsburgh, Phoenix, Flushing, and now we were back in Maryland again. I had learned to work a record player, tell lies, read the funny pages, and feel awkward at parties. But it was not until that morning, in early September 1968, that my story truly began. Until my brother was born, I had no one to tell it to.

When Steve and his wife were about to have their first child, I said to him, "I remember the day we were having our first, and how you were there."

"I was the first one to see her," he said. "After you guys. Not counting the doctors."

"They don't count," I told him.

Then I told him how I remembered his being there, in the LDR at Cedars-Sinai, that day in 1994. My wife was twenty-odd hours into her labor when he showed up, and she had just lost her battle to do the thing without recourse to drugs. My brother showed up around lunchtime, bringing some very good corned beef sandwiches from Jerry's Deli that my wife was not permitted to eat. She railed with some heat against the injustice of this, but then she appeared to take a certain pleasure in the sight of us enjoying them, two brothers slumped identically in plastic chairs, splitting a corned beef on rye. I felt buoyed by the sight of him, too. She was not progressing well, and though despair had by no means set in yet, by the time my brother appeared, it was long since clear to both me and my wife that the labor was not going to be one of the easy ones that you heard about and hoped for. Doctors and nurses were beginning to mutter and make troubling allusions to Pitocin and decelerations and the strain on the baby of a prolonged labor. I could see the fear and the doubt beginning to work their way into my wife's calculation of her chances to have the birth go well, and I hated that sight. I would have given a lot to be able to extinguish or even allay those fears and doubts for a moment. I was trying to be strong and hopeful for her; I was trying to be her hero.

To this end, it was of incalculable value to me to have my brother around. Until the birth of that first child (by cesarian section after thirty-six hours and some scary moments beside the fetal heart monitor), no one but Steve had ever cast my actions in a heroic light, and this was precisely the light that was required. (It also didn't hurt when Steve did that old *M*A*S*H** number of pulling a latex glove halfway down his head and face and puffing it up with exhalations until he looked like some kind of cartoon-balloon rooster.) I made it through the rest of the long afternoon and evening without losing my cool or my faith in my wife to make it through the ordeal to the story at the other side. But when it came time for the baby to be cut from her mother's belly, Steve and I were obliged to part ways.

"You can do it," he said.

I did it. I held my bloody new daughter and gazed into her wide, staring eyes. I spoke to her while they put her under the french-fry lights and drizzled clean water across her peely belly. I assented to the reckoning of her weight and length and learned how to swaddle her in a blanket just like the one in which my brother had ridden home, on our mother's lap, in our family Dodge.

But at some point they had to wheel my wife into the recovery room so she could shake off the nausea and fog of anesthesia enough to meet our child, and I got separated from the helpful nurses, and from my wife, and from my sense of purpose. I found myself dazed, exhausted, and lost, wandering the corridors of Cedars, aimless, clueless, holding in the crook of my right arm a human I did not really know. I kept turning and turning, trying desperately to look as though I knew where I was going and what I was doing. And then I turned a last corner, and ran, almost literally, into Steve.

"Oh my God, Mike," he said, looking into the face of his niece. "I can't believe."

"I know."

"You're a dad."

"Pretty strange," I agreed.

"What happened?" he said, reading my expression, seeing some lingering hollowness of doubt.

"I got a little lost," I said, and I thought of an afternoon with him years before on the Outer Banks of North Carolina.

"Well," he said. "Here we are."

"Here we are."

"Have a seat." He found us a pair of chairs in an alcove off the corridor. "Hold your baby. You're tired."

"Remember that time in Kitty Hawk?" I said. "In the dunes?"

"I remember the dunes," he said. "We were running."

I told him the story of how, when I was sixteen and he was not yet eleven, we had gone down to Nags Head with our mother. The Outer Banks was a place we had visited last when we were small and our parents were still together. On this trip our mother was ensnared deep in the tangles of life as a single woman of the 1970s, and I had just learned how to drive, and in the fall Steve would be leaving to go and live with our father in Pittsburgh, and here, on the sand dunes, we were. In coming to North Carolina, our mother had fled the attentions of a persistent, repeat-calling, fundamentally creepy suitor (today we might call him a stalker) named Francis who, appropriately for a suitor, liked to wear a blue suit, and whom neither of us liked any more than we liked the idea of our mother being troubled by men not our father, or of our soon being separated for a terribly indefinite period by Steve's departure for Pittsburgh. We ran deeper and farther into the dunes, plunging and scrabbling and ass-sledding down their shifting slopes, frightening and delighting ourselves. After a while we lost track of our mother and, hot, weary, I was called upon to lead the way back to her. I had no idea where I was going, or where she might be found, but I let Steve see none of that doubt. I took readings of the sun, and held a moistened finger to the wind, and looked for tracks in the trackless sand. And then we started walking.

"It's like that time," I told him as we searched for our mother. I wanted to keep him occcupied and to conceal the degree of our lostness. "In Pittsburgh."

"Tell me," he said.

I told him the story of how we had decided, one summer afternoon when he was eight and I was fourteen, to walk home to Squirrel Hill from our stepmother's office in the Cathedral of Learning. This was our first joint visit to our father's new hometown, and so far we had never walked alone farther than the four blocks from his house to the Isaly's store on the corner of Forbes and Murray avenues. But we had been driven back and forth a few times between Squirrel Hill and Oakland across the Panther Hollow Bridge, and I had some vague notion of the way. Steve had no idea where anything was, and quite blindly and typically, he put all his faith in me to get us home.

In time I managed to bring us face-to-face with a stretch of asphalt, some patchy-looking trees, and the tall slender stacks of an unmarked, unidentifiable factory of some kind, windowless and fenced. Heat was rising off the asphalt in tall plumes, slicing the mysterious pale factory into long shimmery ribbons. Though I attempted not to show it, I was quite surprised to find us there—

wherever there was—in the enigmatic zone behind the Carnegie Institute. Steve looked to me, awaiting my wisdom, my account of the situation. And though I had no idea where we were, I pointed to the patch of trees and scrub and declared those scrubby trees to constitute Schenley Park. We should walk that way, I told him.

It was a pretty good guess, considering the near-total extent of my ignorance—Schenley Park was actually over there, in that direction, somewhere. We started walking, but somehow or other, I managed to miss the bridge I knew we wanted and brought us instead to a stairway, or rather a concrete landing from which a set of stairs led down into a hollow. There was no obvious way to get up the other side, but it seemed reasonable to me that if stairs went down here, there must be stairs over there that went up. It was a very long stairway down, the steps of concrete, with a railing of painted steel pipe. Indeed, the stairway seemed to lengthen Alice-in-Wonderlandishly as we descended it infinitely; it took us down into a substratum of Pittsburgh that lay even deeper than the dead-bird-filled basement of the Carnegie Museum. We were going down through tangled brambles, climbing vines, and a marvelously thickening growth of blessed shade. That endless stairway got cooler and darker and more silent as the city noises faded away. At the same time, we began to become aware that the strange territory we had discovered was inhabited. There were houses down here, streets, a ball field. From the heights of the stairs it all looked very small and idealized: dollhouses, toy streets, a baseball diamond of green cellophane and modeling clay. We could even see some tiny figures we were eventually able to identify as the native children, children not too different, perhaps, from ourselves, yet adapted to life down here beneath the city. And here we were, Steve and I, exiles from the land of our own childhood, a land of parents who stayed married and families who were not separated by hundreds of miles. We had discovered another lost world, not the irretrievable world of our family but a real one, alive and flourishing and yet somehow mysteriously forgotten.

It turned out that there were all kinds of flaws in my plan to get us home: train tracks to cross, complete with an actual train; a steep, thorny hill up which we were obliged to bushwhack our way, tearing our skin and clothes in the process. In a short story, the character of the younger brother would have been obliged to experience an epiphany about his brother's fallibility, would perhaps see him as having passed irrevocably into the flawed world of adulthood, but Steve just went on trusting me, and following me, and doing what I told him we were going to do, the way he followed me years later on our search for our mother across the dunes of Kitty Hawk.

And then we came upon her along the shore, looking out to sea, her sundress stirring in the breeze, and she turned to us, and for a moment it felt like this was the last summer ever, that life was changing and we were changing, and that everything depended for its preservation on my saying the right thing.

"Look out, Mom," I said, pointing to the nearest line of dunes. "Here comes Francis!"

They both turned, and I laughed, and then we all laughed at

the image of big, soft, harmless Francis in his Clark Kent glasses and his blue suit, trudging up the snaking ridge of those random dunes, 350 miles from home.

"We got lost," Steve told our mother. "Just like that time in Pittsburgh."

"Just like that time in Kitty Hawk," I said, sitting in the corridor of Cedars-Sinai somewhere in the maternity ward.

"You found her," Steve reminded me. "Now what about Ayelet? I bet she wants to hold her daughter."

I stood up, having told him the story he wanted to hear, the one about how I knew what must be done—how I was brave and wily and never really lost, no matter how much it might seem that way.

"Let's go find her," I said.

"But hey, I'm the first one to see you, Sophie," he leaned in to explain to the baby, "after your mom and dad."

I reminded him that I had been the first person to see him after he was born, unless you counted the doctors, and he told me that the doctors don't count.

"I remember," I told him, as the older of my nephews will one day tell his younger brother—his witness, his partner, his inventor, his heart, his courage—the story about the day their story began.

The Ghost of Irene Adler

One summer many years ago, at the Squaw Valley Community of Writers, I gave a reading of a short story of mine called "Millionaires." It's basically the story of Harry and Vince, roommates and best friends, whose long friendship is spoiled when they both fall in love with the same young woman. They have always shared everything—not just housing, books, clothes, and record collections but enthusiasms, manias, and passions. The only thing they have never shared successfully is a girl—not sexually, not emotionally, not at all. All of their individual relationships with women have petered out amid uneasiness and hurt feelings. And yet until this woman Kim comes along, they manage to weather every disruption, their friendship surviving each girl's advent and departure. They have accumulated a small treasury of little mementos and forgotten items, barrettes and bits of jewelry, one for each girlfriend, which they keep on a shelf, almost as a kind of shrine to the durability of their bond with each other, a bond that ultimately, Vince betrays.

I recently ran into an old good friend of mine whom I hadn't seen in years—in the years after our respective marriages, a certain distance had imposed itself—and since then I've found myself thinking about that story, and about the response to my reading it aloud of a young female participant known to history only as Alexis from Texas. Actually, what I might like to talk about is Alexis from Texas, one of those legendary women—the kind Mr. Bernstein recalls in *Citizen Kane*—whom you never forget even though you have nothing, really, to remember. She wore a short black dress, black cowboy boots, and a pair of clunky black Buddy Holly horn-rims (she was the first beautiful woman I ever saw adopt that strategy of inverse enhancement), and when she shot pool, which she did very well, she would cantilever herself way out over the pool table in the breathtaking way of cantilevers everywhere, and one of her long legs would arise behind her as irrepressibly as an accurate new model of the universe, and the skirt of her dress would hike up a couple of inches, and all the guys standing around the pool table would manifest signs of bodily pain.

Anyway, that's all there is to say about Alexis from Texas, except for her criticism of "Millionaires," which, offered as she pumped the cue stick back and forth a few times along the saddle of her thumb, was this: "I liked your story. Everybody knows guys like that. Of course"—sinking her ball with an irrefutable smack and a thud of finality—"it's all about them really being in love with each other."

"Yeah," I said, uncertain. A bit uneasy. "Oh, yeah, you bet."

I swear, this interpretation of Harry and Vince's behavior had never occurred to me. I was just trying, I had thought, to write a story about how a couple of guys—guys like me and my best friend (let's call him Harry)—could share everything, hold everything in common, but a girlfriend. Like, you know, *Jules et Jim*. Did any beautiful young woman ever clean François Truffaut's clock while explaining to him how Jules and Jim were in love only with each other? The problem for Harry and Vince, I thought, was that romantic love was not a thing that could be held at all—collected, curated in a shrine, played with—and thus, it could not be shared. It was unruly, uncontrollable, unreliable, and destructive: a force that in character was opposed to, and in strength, alas (so I probably would have argued at the time), greater than, the force of "simple" friendship.

But I was willing, then and now, to concede that Alexis from Texas had a point. The love between Harry and Vince was the product of sublimated mutual physical attraction. It was also the expression of a mutual sympathy, an affinity that had nothing, and could have nothing, to do with sex; it was beyond sex and yet no match for it. Maybe love was a kind of force or radiation that, like light, should be understood as both wave and particle.

Almost twenty years later, having seen a number of friendships come and go, for all kinds of reasons and for no reason at all, I think Alexis from Texas and I missed the real point of the story, or rather, I left out of my story the reason that a friendship between men most often falters, fades, and dies when a woman— *the* Woman, in Sherlock Holmes's formulation—intrudes. Yes, sure, sometimes both guys fall in love with her, like Harry and

Vince, or Jules and Jim, or Brad Pitt and Aidan Quinn in that movie with everybody wearing buffalo-hide coats and smoldering at one another; and a lot of the time, on some level, it's not really the girl they each want to do, or not only the girl. But most of the time, pace Alexis and the author of "Millionaires," what happens is that one guy's girl—the wife, as things with the Woman usually turn out—just really gets on the other guy's nerves. And strangely, he gets on hers.

She has no understanding of Pavement; she won't—won't—eat even mildly spiced Indian food, let alone the vindaloo at Biki's that, when you finish it, leaves you bald with a ring of hair lying around the legs of your chair; she hates baseball, believes in astrology (oh, so he's a triple Gemini, guess that explains the third nipple), got him to go snowboarding (Him. On a snowboard. In one of those little llama hats with the earflaps), to decorate his living room with angels, and to give a shit about women's issues and the Planet, of all things; and worst of all, most egregious of all, you cannot believe the way she talks to him. No, worst of all: You can't believe that he puts up with it.

At first glance this appears to be merely a subspecies of a greater failure, one that ultimately explains almost all the ills and wrongnesses of the world, cataclysmic and trivial. I mean the failure of imagination. And I suspect that when a male friendship dies over a woman, the failure of imagination is to blame. But for once—just this once—I might be tempted to argue that in this case the failure of imagination is not entirely our fault, not entirely the product of our inveterate human tendency toward withholding or bankrupting the faculty of imagination at the very moment when it is most required. When the Woman enters the life of the Holmes to whom you have always served as Watson, and vice versa, it's not simply that you can't or won't imagine what he sees in her. It's that you aren't meant to understand; you have not touched to the innermost core of another person and hence the zero limits of imagination.

That's what gives the process of losing a friendship over a woman such a lasting sense of distress and confusion: The loss obliges you to confront the fundamental mystery of another man, one whom you believed you knew as well as you knew yourself. But there is something in the guy, something crucial and irreducible, that you do not understand at all, and She is the proof. You have no access to that innermost kernel of him, and you never did. And in turn, this leads you to question everything you ever thought you knew, not only about him but about the man you thought you knew as well as you knew your best friend—yourself.

Because after all, look who you chose—look at your Irene Adler. You and your best friend fell in together, laid your collections on the table and traded for duplicates, found each other amid the slim pickings in life's great battalion of idiots, made friends. You chose each other, but the Woman was chosen for you, bonded to you through the actions of some mysterious agency that, however much you and she might have in common, however much you enjoy birding together, or watching The Wire or Peter Greenaway movies, or co-reigning as duke and consort of your local chapter of the Society for Creative Anachronism, has nothing to do with any of that. This agency operates as forcefully, and binds with as much upheaval, as much power and delight and comfort and destructiveness, when two lovers have nothing in common.

What became of that friendship is what became of your heart in love: You lost it. And once it's gone—friendship, heart—you never get it all back. That's what makes her *the* Woman; that's what makes the keeping of an old friend through all the vicissitudes of love and fortune such a rare and wonderful or an empty and terrible thing. Either you and your old friend encountered the black box at each other's core, with its scatter of mystery particles on which the invisible forces of love and fate operate, and by some miraculous luck, you imagined or muddled your way past, beyond, or around that mystery; or, tragically, you were never obliged to encounter it at all.

The Heartbreak Kid

One night when I was nineteen or twenty, I sat drinking Rolling Rock beer and smoking marijuana in an artfully squalid Squirrel Hill apartment with a friend who liked to get drunk and stoned and tell you what was wrong with you and what you ought and ought not to expect from a life such as yours. That probably meets the legal definition of an asshole, but I liked the guy, and his opinion meant a lot to me. "Joe the Lion," I called him, after the Bowie song (*A couple of drinks / on the house / and he was / a fortune teller he said / nail me to my car / and I'll tell you who you are*). "You have no *tristeza*" was his diagnosis of me on this particular evening. "And you never will." He was not a Spaniard or a Mexican. He was not a native speaker of Spanish at all. A Pittsburgh kid, Slovak on his mother's side. But I believed he knew what he was talking about—he spoke with unfeignable authority, and his words haunted me afterward for a very long time.

Tristeza means sadness, and common sense would suggest that I ought to have been pleased with his analysis of my life and fate.

But he seemed to hold my lack of sadness against me or, rather, to pity me for that lack, and it was not long before I began to regret the absence of *tristeza* in my soul or destiny. I was by nature (whatever that means) a cheerful person, born into comfortable circumstances during a time of unprecedented plenty, free, male, able-bodied, reasonably clever, fortunate, and willing to work. Socially, things for me had been a bit rough there for a while, but over the past few years I had been doing better in that regard. I had fallen in love, gotten laid, made friends with interesting people who understood the world in terms of abstract Spanish concepts. Now it turned out that I was suffering from a grievous lack of *tristeza*.

Actually, I was all right with the idea—how could I deny it?—that I was not then in possession of a usable quantity of heroic sadness. It was the part about my never getting hold of any *tristeza* that rankled me.

My upbringing and the thing called my nature had accustomed me to thinking that if I applied myself and took advantage of my opportunities, there was nothing I might want to become or possess that I could not. Without saying anything to my friend—without ever announcing my intentions to anyone, least of all to myself—I set out to remedy this grave deficit of heartbreak or, as I understood it, of the aura, the ineradicable residue, of heartbreak. I implemented a crash program and, like a middle-tier regional power seeking weapons-grade plutonium, went out and got myself a broken heart.

A study of the available literature—or part of it, since the available literature occupied half the world's library shelves and three fourths of the attention of its poets—seemed to suggest that one indispensable precursor to the production of *tristeza* was regret. There were others—grief, exile, loss—and along the way, I might reasonably expect to acquire them or at least get a few leads on their whereabouts. But regret was the one prerequisite for heart-break that I could hope to ensure a steady supply of. All I needed to do was start making mistakes, but I must do so diligently and clearly, taking full advantage of all my opportunities. I must put my trust in unreliable people, take on responsibilities I could not hope to discharge, count on impossible outcomes, ignore blessings that were right under my nose while expending my youth and energy in the pursuit of dubious pleasure. I must court disappointment, miscalculate, lie when the truth would serve better and tell the truth when the kindest thing would be to tell a lie. Above all, I would have to stick to a course of action long after it was clearly revealed to be wrong.

A year passed in much the same way as those that had preceded it, and although I had gotten into difficulties and hurt people's feelings, lost money, and wasted time, I remained more or less the same cheerful and fortunate person I always had been, not unduly prone to regret, with nothing to grieve and everything still to lose. I had cheated on one girlfriend and been cheated on by another. I had done incredibly stupid things, such as buy gum sticks of hash-ish from unknown Africans on a scary street in Paris called Rue de l'Ouest. Finally, I had removed myself from the company of Joe the Lion and all my other friends and lovers, decamped to California, and holed up in a rented room in Berkeley. I had started work on a novel that would display to the world the depth and understanding of my sorrowing soul, and at night sometimes I would lie in my room feeling alone and friendless and contemplate the ache in me with a distinct sense of anticipatory pleasure, like a child watching his lima bean sprout on a damp paper towel in a dish.

That fall I began graduate school at UC Irvine, in the MFA writing program. There was a girl I used to see around the English department sometimes, a cute blonde with a gamine face and a Jean Seberg haircut, plump lips, snub nose, big eyes, an air of being fun to be around. One day I saw her, or thought I saw her, in the restaurant of the old student union. She was getting up from the table where she had been chatting with some friends, and as she carried her tray to the trash, I decided to go over and say hi.

I'm not sure how long it took—not more than a few seconds—for me to realize that this was the other blond gamine of a PhD candidate in the Irvine English Department. I had seen her before and had confused her before with her colleague. She was not as pretty as the other girl, and in place of the other's slightly hardened pertness, she wore a doubtful, cautious half-smile, as if she knew you intended, like the rest of the world, to try to put one over on her, but she was hip to you, she was on to your methods. People had tricked her and deceived her and let her down in a number of ways, and it had left her embittered and a little punchy. She was older than me by seven years, and probably no wiser, but she knew enough, at least, to be on her guard.

It turned out she lived on the Balboa Peninsula, where I was living at the time, and she was just about to head home in her worn old Toyota hatchback. Did I maybe want to catch a ride?

She had a big nose and strong legs and eyes that were an unusual shade of golden green, as pale as champagne—and sad; she was a pretty unhappy girl. I looked at her, this woman who was not the one I wanted to talk to, and I wasn't even sure if I really liked her much. I remember thinking, as I stood there weighing her offer, *This is going to be a mistake.*

"Sure," I said. "That'd be great."

Eighteen months later, I married her on the back lawn of her parents' house in Seattle. It was, in a way that I found almost intoxicating—the way slamming a trunk lid on your hand or missing a step as you climb a stairway in the dark can be intoxicating—a great mistake.

I did like her, as it turned out. She had an eye for furniture and flowers, a rich history of weird sex, weird jobs, and weird scenes, an ear for quirky pop tunes. I found that you could make her intensely happy for a little while with a handful of sweet peas or by putting her in a dinghy and handing her a pair of good binoculars and sending her out very early to row softly among the coots and the buffleheads. Most important for me, she had expectations of how a man ought to act and speak and shoulder his obligations, and in the three years of our marriage, I learned how to be a husband.

But she was often miserable—sometimes justifiably, usually

for no reason at all—and in a short period of time, I found that I was miserable, too. There were operatic arguments, all-night ransackings of the contents of our souls, drunken vituperations, migraines, rages, grim gray bitter mornings. We traveled, and moved, and bought a house and acquired animals, and engaged in all the standard ploys and dodges, short of having children (thank God), employed by couples trying to outrun the shadow of that first enduring mistake. The first wrong kiss, the first broken fuck, the first harsh word, the first false apology, the first slap and fiery imprint of a hand on a cheek.

Then one spring night I found myself fleeing the house we had bought in all our desperate and mistaken hope for some kind of future together. There had been shouting and tears and a decision to maybe, maybe really, take a little time off. I was steering my car through the rain along a country highway on an island near Seattle, and it was getting dark. It had been raining for days, weeks, months. I had a tape in the player of Te Kanawa singing "Un bel di vedremo," and there was something about the dreamy stretch of road, the gray light of dusk, the throb of grief in the voice of the singer, the helpless hopelessness of the song, and the long hard stretch behind me of months and years of living with the consequences of my mistake. Something inside me broke, and my face was wet with tears.

I remembered Joe the Lion then, and his prediction that night years before. *If he could see me now,* I thought to myself. Then I turned off the music, and opened the window, and let the rain come into the car. I drove to the island's one town. I stopped at the market and bought myself an ice-cream sandwich and sat in the car with the ball game on the radio. At some point I realized, to my horror, that I was perfectly content. I passed a few minutes working my way around the edges of the ice-cream sandwich with my tongue, listening as a wondrous rookie named Ken Griffey Jr. caught the admiration of the announcer and the crowd; just sitting there, fulfilling my terrible destiny.

A Gift

On my twenty-eighth birthday, I got a package from my father, a small padded Jiffy envelope containing two neat little bundles wrapped in white tissue paper, folded and pleated and sealed up in their pouch with the slightly neurotic precision that is characteristic of my father and that he inherited, I believe, from his mother, Irene, who wrapped everything, even the unpeeled oranges on her kitchen counter and the silverware in her drawer. He'd neglected to include a note or a card. I unwrapped the first neat little bundle and found, in their clear plastic sleeves, four baseball cards printed by the Bowman Gum company in 1952, the year my father was fourteen. There was a Bobby Adams, and a Billy Goodman, and two pitchers named Howie, Judson and Pollet. I consider myself a baseball fan and a moderately accomplished student of baseball history, but I confess that I had never heard of any of these players. Thinking that I had inadvertently opened the "auxiliary" portion of my birthday present—perhaps some duplicate cards of my father's (he's a collector) that he had thrown in as a kind of bonus—I tore open the other bundle and found three more cards, also Bowmans, also in their archival plastic PVC-free sleeves: a Mickey Harris, and a Vern Bickford, and then a Randy Gumpert.

Despite the note of faintly derisive disappointment inherent in any sentence that ends in the word *Gumpert*, I was not at all disappointed in my father's gift. The 1952 Bowman cards are among the most serenely beautiful exemplars of a popular art form not notable, it must be admitted, for works of great beauty, serene or otherwise. The baseball card has generally and throughout its hundred-odd-year history been an object supremely suited for insertion into the spokes of a bicycle wheel. Though to the true fan, any awkward old photograph of some square-jawed, wall-eyed fellow named Carlton Molesworth in a peaked beanie, staring off into the outfield on some long-gone sepia afternoon, may have a kind of poignant charm, and though some of the cards of the thirties and forties, such as National Chicle's Diamond Star and those issued by the Leaf Gum Company, have a kind of flat, primary-colored crudeness that makes them resemble so many tiny Warhols, most baseball cards are, as specimens of the photographic and design arts, at best uninteresting to look at and, far more frequently, outright ugly.

The 1952 Bowmans are different: Accidentally, perhaps, they attain a cool and evocative beauty. For one thing, there is no printed text on the obverse of the card, no goofy bird or Injun or sock; there is only a small simulated autograph—say, "Randall P. Gumpert"—modest, dignified, perfectly legible, stitched across

the portrait of the Boston right-hander. And the portraits themselves! The ballplayers have been depicted not in the usual glum
mug shots, nor in the clumsy hand-drawn caricatures found on
cards of earlier years, but in an odd combination of painting and
photograph, photographs not merely tinted and retouched but
painted over, transformed. Bloodred Boston B's on caps, radium-
white uniforms, dreamy powder-blue textbook skies—all the
colors run rich and surreal; the lace cornices of Yankee Stadium
over the shoulder of Randall P. Gumpert are a luminous cake-icing
green, his resolute mouth a jet-black cartoon line; and one feels
that these are unquestionably idealized paintings of ballplayers.
But all the men have been caught in mid-windup, or after letting
fly, or stooping to short-hop a grounder, as only a photograph can
catch a man with his mouth open, or his teeth clenched, or his
forehead furrowed in candid anxiety over the location of this next
pitch, or with his thoughts patently elsewhere, his eyes looking
strangely lost and vacant the way eyes can in photographs.

And then, inexorably, you turn the card over. Because the great
secret theme of baseball is Loss (with its teammate, Failure), reading the backs of baseball cards is always an exercise in pity, and
this is particularly true of the reverse of an older card like a 1952
Bowman, where the details of a ballplayer's career are usually given
not in the clean, bloodless statistical charts of today but in terse
prose paragraphs, where they take on some of the mighty sadness
of narrative, and each card can become the tiniest of novels whose
plot is the familiar tale of futility and squandered promise and a
ballclub's giving up. Howie Pollet "began the 1951 season with the

Cards. In 6 games for them, with no wins and 3 losses. With the Pirates Howie took the mound 21 times, with 6 wins and 10 losses. Season's record: 6 and 13. Led League in 1946 with 21 wins. Had 20 wins in 1949. Broke into majors with Cardinals." At the bottom of every card is the send-away offer of a baseball cap of your favorite major league team ("a $1.00 value") for five waxed wrappers and fifty cents.

The thing was, I didn't really collect baseball cards, and I thought my father knew that. During the winter of the Lockout of 1990, just before my first marriage ended, in the miserable grip of a Seattle January that consisted, without exaggeration, of thirty full days of rain, I had dabbled in the hobby out of a kind of desperate yearning for a season that, it then appeared, might not have its Opening Day. But I've never had the collecting temperament—not the way my father has it—and when the package arrived, over a year had passed since I had bought my last card. But that wasn't important. I owned a little-used copy of Dr. Beckett's Price Guide, in which I could look up the values of the seven cards and see that my father's gift was a generous one, but that wasn't important, either. That was what I was thinking, at any rate, as I took down the copy of *Macmillan's Baseball Encyclopedia* that had been my father's birthday gift to me in 1970, and I discovered that Billy Goodman was actually a pretty good ballplayer who in 1950 led the American League in hitting with a .354 average, and that Vern Bickford, in the same year, pitched the season's only no-hitter. It wasn't important that I didn't collect 1952 Bowmans nor care what they were worth (not really), or that when I was finished turning each card over and over and wondering at that lost expression in Howie Pollet's eyes, I would put them all away in my sock drawer and "lose" them for many years (they recently turned up again, ageless in their Mylar jackets). The important thing was the nature of the gift, was my father's saying to me after twenty-eight years during which we had lost Roberto Clemente and our beloved Washington Senators and my father's mother and father, and had split two divorces between us, and had known all the usual guilt and bitterness and recrimination, and had moved, in modern and terrible fashion, to opposite ends of the continent, "Here, son, have seven baseball cards." What's important was that baseball, after all these years of artificial turf and expansion and the designated hitter and drugs and free agency and thousand-dollar bubble-gum cards, is still a gift given by fathers to sons.

[V]

STYLES OF MANHOOD

Faking It

At one time there was a pair of hooks on the back of the bathroom door from which one could hang a couple of towels, but people used the towels as vines, webbing, and rope for games of Tarzan, Spider-Man, and Look! I'm a Dead Guy That Hung Themself, and now, to serve four children, there remained one wall-mounted towel rack with only two bars. This situation encouraged the general tendency among the children to leave their soggy bath towels in Noguchi-like arrangements on the floor. The parents allocated resources for a pilot program of nag-based maintenance, targeted yelling, and regular exercises in stumbling over damp bath towels in dark bedrooms, but when emotional funding at last ran out, it became apparent that someone would have to put up a second towel rack. Responsibility for this task logically fell to the person who knew, kind of, how to use an electric drill.

You should have seen me. I had my cordless Makita in its blue high-impact plastic case. I had a ratcheting screwdriver, a nice Sears Craftsman hammer, a mechanical pencil with a good eraser, and (that most beautifully named of all tools) a spirit level. I sat down on the tile floor of the bathroom with the new chrome towel rack from Restoration Hardware and its gnomic instruction sheet, and I ran the fingers of one hand across the designated stretch of beadboard while sagely stroking my whiskers with the fingers of the other. I strongly suspect that I may well have looked as if I knew what I was doing.

I managed to sustain the appearance of competence over nearly the entire course of the next three hours, except for the painful minute that followed my dropping one of the metal towel bars onto my right thumb, behind whose nail, like a ghost on an old television screen, a grayish-blue blotch immediately made manifest. But from the moment I began to trace with my pencil the prospective outline of one of the faceplates against the beadboard until the moment when, holding my breath, I insinuated two ominously heavy towels into the works of the now-mounted towel rack, I was expecting, at every instant, disaster: molly bolts sliding with a creak of splintering wood from their holes, nickel-plated towel bars clanging against the floor.

I knew how to use my tools, more or less. I understood the rudimentary physics of tension and load that were supposed to hold the rack together and keep it fixed to the wall. And yet on both the deepest and the most practical levels, I had no reason to believe, no evidence from prior experience of myself, physics, or life itself, that I knew how or would be able to pull off the job. In fact, I had encountered a certain amount of tragedy in my dealings with molly bolts over the years.

"You're going to put that up?" my wife had asked me when I brought the rack home from the store. She didn't sound dubious so much as surprised, as if I were also proposing to weave a new set of bath towels from cotton I had grown and harvested myself.

"Duh," I said coolly. "No biggie."

This is an essential element of the business of being a man: to flood everyone around you in a great radiant arc of bullshit, one whose source and object of greatest intensity is yourself. To behave as if you have everything firmly under control even when you have just sailed your boat over the falls. "To keep your head," wrote Rudyard Kipling in his classic poem "If," which articulated the code of high-Victorian masculinity in whose fragmentary shadow American men still come of age, "when all about you are losing theirs"; but in reality, the trick of being a man is to give the appearance of keeping your head when, deep inside, the truest part of you is crying out, *Oh, shit!*

Perhaps in the end there is little difference between keeping one's head and appearing to do so; perhaps the effort required to feign unconcern and control over a situation itself imparts a measure of control. If so, then the essence of traditional male virtue lies in imposture, in an ongoing act of dissimulation—fronting—which hardly conforms to the classic Kipling model of square-dealing candor.

I have no doubt that the male impulse to downplay his own lack of fitness for a job, to refuse to acknowledge his inadequacy, insufficiency, or lack of preparation, has been and continues to be responsible for a large share of the world's woes, in the form of the accidents, errors, and calamities that result from specific or overarching acts of faking it, a grim encyclopedia of which the G. W. Bush administration readily affords. There is also the more subtle damage that is done repeatedly to boys who grow up learning from their fathers and the men around them the tragic lesson that failure is not a human constant but a kind of aberration of gender, a flaw in a man, to be concealed.

Men's refusal to stop and ask for directions, a foundational cliché of women's criticism, analysis, and stand-up mockery of male behavior, is a perfect example of this tendency to put up a front, in that it views as aberrant a condition—being lost—that is ineluctable, a given of human existence. We are born lost and spend vast stretches of our lives on wrong turns and backtracking. In this respect, male fronting resembles a number of other behaviors typically ascribed to men and masculinity, in that it proceeds by denying essential human conditions or responses—say public displays of mutual affection, grief, or triumph—marking them as feminine, infantile, socially unacceptable.

I learned to pretend that I know what I am doing from my own father, an extremely intelligent and well-informed man whose intermittent bouts with mistakenness and inaccuracy visibly cost him bitter pain and embarrassment, and shocked the hell out of me when I was a child. By fiat and consensus, fathers are always right, so that when facts or events inevitably conspire to prove them wrong, they and their sons alike totter on the brink of an abyss. I have never forgotten the day—I can't have been older than five—when I watched in silent horror as my father, imperturbable and confident and disdaining the instruction sheet, assembled an entire barbecue grill with its key pieces upside down and backward. I remember my mounting anxiety about whether I should point out his mistake to him, and most clearly of all I remember the sharp and mocking look my mother gave him when at last I betrayed him.

When I became a father, I made a promise to myself not to pretend to knowledge I did not possess, not to claim authority I plainly lacked, not to hide my doubts and uncertainties, my setbacks and regrets, from my children. And so I have tried to share them over the years as I have been fired from screenwriting jobs or proved wrong or led to look a fool. I have made a point (until the recent advent of GPS) to stop and ask for directions. But sometimes I waver in my resolve. My sense of myself as a father, my sense of fathers, is so deeply caught up with some kind of primal longing (which I think we all share) for inerrancy, for the word of God, for a rock and a redeemer, a mighty hand and an outstretched arm, for the needle that always always finds true north in a storm.

And maybe that longing in one's wife and children runs beyond the understanding of even the most painfully self-conscious of fathers. One recent winter my family and I found ourselves stuck in Jackson Hole, Wyoming, in the middle of a snowstorm. All flights out were canceled. There was a flight home from Idaho Falls, a drive of two hours through a high mountain pass, or three hours by an easier route that skirted the mountains. Either way, there would be snow, ice, unknown chances. If we wanted, we could wait for an airline-chartered bus that might eventually depart for

Idaho Falls, getting us home to Oakland no one could say when. Or we could sit tight, wait it out, and hope to get home sometime tomorrow or the next day.

I didn't give it a moment's thought. We had rented a big strong four-by-four. It had the tires and the muscle for the roads up there. I liked the way I felt behind its wheel, competent and unperturbed by weather. The fact that I had not driven in a blizzard in twenty years barely entered the conscious register of my thoughts.

"Let's drive," I told my wife. "I'll go the long way around."

She looked at me with a strange expression, then said okay; later, after we had made it safely and without incident up and down through ice and rain and snowfall that was at times blinding, my wife told me that she initially thought I was dangerously insane when I proposed driving to Idaho Falls through a blizzard. But then she had heard something in my voice that reassured her; she'd seen something in my eyes. I looked as if I knew what I was doing. And though I gripped the wheel with bloodless hands and prayed wildly to the gods of the interstate trucker whom I carefully tailed all the way to Idaho, in the backseat the kids calmly watched their iPod videos, and my wife studied the map and gossiped with me, and none of them knew or suspected for a moment—for I never betrayed, by word or deed, my secret—that I was in way over my head. I was the father and the husband; they were safe with me. We made it to the airport right on time to catch the next flight home.

"I knew you could do it," my wife said, and I thought about saying, "Well, that makes one of us." But I held my tongue and nodded with a Kiplingesque modesty, because the truth was that in the absence of any evidence or experience or reason to think so, I had known that I could do it, too. I had no choice, do you see, but to know that.

By the way, the towels are still hanging from the rack in the bathroom. And I fully expect, at any moment, in the dead of night, to hear a telltale clatter on the tiles.

Art of Cake

My life as a cook began on the back panel of a Bisquick box, with Velvet Crumb Cake. This was shortly before my tenth birthday. By that time I'd been helping my mother in the kitchen for several years, as she had helped her own mother, Nettie Cohen. Through helping her—and I know just how patience-taxing and supremely unhelpful a young sous chef can be—I had learned the basic techniques and tools to use: how to level a cup of flour, chop an onion, work the Mixmaster, separate an egg. But I don't remember preparing any particular dish until I undertook the recipe on the back of that bright yellow box.

Bisquick mix was an anonymous staple of my mother's kitchen. Pancakes and biscuits were never made with anything else, and nothing else was ever made with it. I think that was the initial appeal of the idea of Velvet Crumb Cake. I was shocked to discover that Bisquick had other uses, other roles that it had been waiting to play, like a shy yet talented understudy. The realization was like finding out that I could make a working model of an

X-15 rocket plane out of a rubber-band glider. The only Bisquick recipes I'd ever seen were the two printed on a floury and tattered square of cardboard that my mother had cut from the back of an old box years before and then abandoned to her special Bisquick canister—ordered by mail from Betty Crocker—to be buried and reburied in an endless drift of biscuit mix. For years I never saw a Bisquick box at all. The chance revelation of the possibility of Velvet Crumb Cake, with its extravagant name, seemed to hint at the existence of a world hidden within the world of our kitchen, and to hold out promise of a more fabulous one beyond.

It was coffee cake; I hope that statement implies no sense of disappointment. Eaten warm from the oven, moist and crumbly, a nice coffee cake is pretty hard to fault. Coffee cake! I had made a coffee cake! Mysteriously, I thought, it contained no coffee. The velvet crumb business turned out to revolve around an impasto of butter, brown sugar, chopped nuts, flaked coconut, and a little milk that you spread over the cake after it came out of the oven. Then you stuck it back in the oven for a minute or two. Something wonderful happened to those five ingredients when you blended them and briefly subjected them to intense heat. The result was both smooth and grainy, crisp and chewy. Cooking, it turned out, was a magical act, a feat of transformation, a way of turning the homely and the familiar into something finer, like carving a pumpkin into a lantern.

That year for my birthday my mother gave me a cookbook. It was called *Betty Crocker's New Boys and Girls Cook Book*. Like the Bisquick box, its cover was bright yellow. It featured intensely colored photographs of the things you could make from it: huge, lustrous cakes, casseroles, and molds awesome as monuments in a depopulated landscape. The recipe for spaghetti called (in retrospect, somewhat nauseatingly) for you to boil the noodles in the tomato sauce. A lot of the other recipes given in *Betty Crocker's New Boys and Girls Cook Book*, perhaps not surprisingly, suggested that they be prepared with Betty Crocker–brand ingredients, especially Bisquick. Many turned for their effects on bits of kitchen legerdemain, exploiting quirks of food chemistry. I was fascinated by and still recall affectionately a recipe for Fudge Upside-Down Cake (or something like that—my copy disappeared years ago) that went into the oven with the batter on the bottom of the cake pan, under a layer of boiling water, and emerged with a layer of cake on top, floating like the earth's mantle on a glutinous brown magma.

My mother was into cookbooks, and as soon as she saw my interest, she gave me the run of her library and let me try to make pretty much whatever sounded good. It was a solid and typical American-cookbook shelf of the day: keystones like the *Better Homes and Gardens New Cook Book* and *Joy of Cooking*; Julia Child and Craig Claiborne; an intimidating bunch of classical French compendia; and period novelties like *365 Ways to Cook Hamburger* and a fondue cookbook. The Library of Babel that is ethnic cuisine was summarized in a footnote, Claiborne's *New York Times International Cookbook*. My all-time favorite, from the moment of its publication in 1972, was James Beard's *American Cookery*. It had a recipe for nearly everything an American kid could ever imagine eating, including squirrel. Almost in passing—rather, in the style of my mother—it taught the fundamentals of the kitchen: how to boil shrimp, poach an egg, prepare an artichoke. (It also offered excellent recipes for pancakes and for biscuits, including those of Beard's own mother.) And in retelling the history of the United States from Indian pudding to cheeseburgers, through the history of our great cookbooks and cooks (most of them women), it also turned out to be a kind of autobiography in the form of recipes, written in prose that was magisterial and laconic. I used to lie around reading it for hours.

I had a lot of disasters in the kitchen, even during the long period when I was cooking under my mother's supervision and with the benefit of her experience. I still fail all the time, in particular when I turn to baking. After hundreds of attempts, following dozens of different formulas, I don't think I have ever made what I would consider to be a completely successful pie crust. Disaster is somehow part of the appeal of cooking for me. If that first Velvet Crumb Cake had turned out a flop, I don't know if I would have pursued my interest in cooking. But cooking entails stubbornness and a tolerance—maybe even a taste—for last-minute collapse. You have to be able to enjoy the repeated and deliberate following of a more or less lengthy, more or less complicated series of steps whose product is very likely—after all that work, with no warning, right at the end—to curdle, sink, scorch, dry up, congeal, burn, or simply taste bad.

This may form part of the male aspect of cookery, a pursuit that combines three classic male modes of gratification: the mastering of an arcane lore bound up in accumulable tomes; mindless repetition (the thing that leads boys to take up card tricks, free-throw shooting, video games); and the staking of everything on a last throw of the dice. Cooking satisfies the part of me that enjoys struggling for days to transfer an out-of-print vinyl record by Klaatu to digital format, screwing with scratch filters and noise reducers, only to have the burn fail every time at the very same track. I'm not at all saying a woman cook doesn't feel the identical mad urge to keep ruining the same dish over and over until she gets it right. I'm just saying that every woman I've ever known has mocked me for being that way.

A few years after Velvet Crumb Cake entered my life, I was obliged to consider an aspect of cooking that has traditionally been thought of as female: that of feeding my family. When I was fourteen, my mother, holding a brand-new law degree from the University of Baltimore, went to work at a federal agency in Washington, D.C., a job that obliged her to rise early and commute almost an hour each way. By the time she arrived home at night, she had neither the energy nor the imagination to make dinner for my brother and me. "If you want to eat a nice hot dinner every night," she told me, proposing to raise my allowance to a then-hefty fifteen dollars a week, "you're going to have to cook it yourself."

So that was what I did—every night for the next four years, until I left for college. I learned to cook all of the homely dishes that my mother had made for us all my life: Swiss steak, spaghetti and meatballs, baked chicken, lasagna, stir-fry, matzo-ball soup, brisket and kasha, beef and macaroni, breaded flounder, beef stew, chicken-fried steak. A number of these recipes were my grand-mother's, and they reflected the nature and history of my mother's family—Jewish, southern (she was born and raised in Virginia and Maryland), and midcentury assimilationist in the best sense of the word: absorbing other cultural traditions as much as it was itself absorbed. I cooked when I felt like it and when I did not, when there was no risk of ruining anything and very little of interest in the recipe once I had mastered it. I cooked for people who were not always hungry, not always appreciative or amazed, not always in the mood for the lamb chop on their plate.

When I married my wife, had children, and began to cook for them, after many footloose years of recondite kitchen experimentation with the gods of chic vegetarianism, of ethnic-cuisine purism, and of the pasta machine, with non-cow cheeses and sun-dried vegetables and edible flowers, I inevitably sought help, even a kind of instruction, in those recipes from the *American Cookery* of my mother's kitchen. I incorporated more modern dishes and ingredients into my regular repertoire, and I acquired many, many new cookbooks, but when it was time to get serious about feeding my family, there was not much doubt about where to turn. A fair portion of the three-by-five cards in my recipe box are written in my mother's hand, and the thing is bulging with folded-up sheets of her typed instructions for Sour Cream Nut Cake or Chicken Rose.

This turns out to be the enduring source of the pleasure I find in the kitchen. It's the one that was there from the start, even before my chance encounter with the glories of a velvety crumble of caramelized bliss on the top of a biscuit-mix cake: the connection to my mother, who not only fed her children well but taught me how to feed my own just the way her mother had taught her. In his great work, James Beard somewhat radically positioned himself as the heir and celebrant of a long line of American woman cooks, from Miss Leslie to Fannie Farmer to his own mother, and there must have been something in this unexpected male affirmation of female inheritance that registered with me.

I grew up during a time of dissolving boundaries, shifting economies, loosened definitions of male and female, of parent and child. Without shame or stigma, a marriage could be allowed to come undone, a woman could become a lawyer and go out and earn a good living. And a boy could take to the kitchen, the center of every home, and find there a sense of history and connectedness to anchor him, something that would not disappear or blow away or change beyond recognition. The processes of the kitchen, the secret chemistry that underlies the magical Velvet Crumb transformation of sugar by heat, are unchanging. Even if we can't always master them, they are constant and true. Incidentally, these are qualities shared by my mother. That tumultuous era, and the new conditions of family life it imposed, obliged me to try to be like her in some measure. I'm lucky that it also permitted me to feel it was all right to want to be, even though I was a boy.

On Canseco

Before I start arguing that it's muddleheaded and misses the point to disparage the greatness of a baseball player for his want of goodness as a man—before I rise to the defense of Jose Canseco—let me begin by offering one example of my own muddleheadedness in this regard. A big part of what I have always admired about the late Roberto Clemente as a ballplayer is what a good, strong, thoughtful man he seems to have been; his stoic dignity in the face of ignorance and bigotry; how he died while trying to help the victims of a great disaster, etc. I choose to view Clemente's grace on the field as reflecting and reflected by the graceful way in which he conducted his public life (when one has demonstrably nothing to do with the other) and both together as lasting proof of some private gracefulness as a man, when I have no way of ever knowing what form the true, secret conduct of his life may have taken. I have no idea what Clemente's relationship was to drugs, or what his feelings would have been about performance enhancers like anabolic steroids, but I would like to think that he would have viewed them both with disfavor, and that he was faithful to his wife, temperate in his habits, and modest about his accomplishments. Yes, I would like to think that, because I'm just foolish and mistaken enough to think that great baseball players must also be good men.

There is no question that Jose Canseco was sometimes a great baseball player. If you have any doubt about that, you weren't paying attention to Canseco on the days during the seasons when he paid attention to the game, and that's hard to imagine since, like Clemente, the man arrested the eye of the spectator, held the attention like a shard of mirror dangling from a wire in the sunshine, even when he was just standing around waiting for something to happen. But I'm not going to get into that here. The question of Canseco's greatness or lack thereof can be debated endlessly, with statistics and anecdotes to support both sides, and some of us will never understand why Ron Santo, Gil Hodges, and Dick Allen are not in the Baseball Hall of Fame while others, many of whom serve on the hall's Veterans Committee, always seem to vote to keep them out. And God knows I have no intention of claiming that Jose Canseco qualifies as a good man, according to the conventions of my own garden-variety morality of consistent effort, altruism, and personal integrity defined as the keeping of one's promises to other people. Canseco's want of goodness on those terms is also arguable, I suppose, though not by me. But I will go out on a limb and venture that any list of the one hundred greatest baseball players who ever lived would conform to the pattern for our species, and therefore contain a sizable number of men who spent most of their lives fumbling with an inherent tendency to shirk, ignore the sufferings of others, tell lies, and evade responsibility. Playing baseball well does not make you a better person any more than writing well does. The illusion that lures us into the error of confounding Clemente's goodness as a man with his greatness as a ballplayer is that when a man is playing baseball well, as when a man is writing well, he seems to himself in that moment to be a better person than he is. He puts it all together, he has all the tools, in a way that seems impossible outside the lines of the ball field or the margins of the page. He shines, and we catch the reflected glint of that and extend the shining one an overall credit for luminosity that almost nobody could merit. Clemente, I think, shone with the grace and integrity of his play even when he was not on the field.

In other words, Roberto Clemente was a hero, and Jose Canseco, by this definition, is not. By his own admission, Canseco has shirked responsibilities and hurt people and lied and broken a lot of promises, large and small. And used steroids. Therefore, many people seem to feel he is not to be admired, neither in the past, during his brief heyday—so that we must retroactively rescind our delight in his style and our amazement at his prowess, put an asterisk beside our memory of the pleasure of his company over the course of a few long summers—nor in the present, not even when he steps forward to tell the truth, a big, meaningful, dolorous truth that most of us, measured by our own standards of heroism, would have a hard time bringing ourselves to tell. Canseco can't possibly be a hero to anyone—he laid down that burden many years and arrests and screwups ago—and furthermore (goes the rap), there is nothing remotely admirable about Canseco's allegation of widespread inveterate use of steroids by himself and by ballplayers such as Mark McGwire, who have a readier claim on our admiration and shoulder more naturally its weight.

In breaking the code of silence on steroid use, we have been informed by sportswriters, by commentators, and by his former teammates, opponents, and coaches, Canseco was only out for money. If lying would have paid better than telling the truth, then Canseco would have lied (indeed, some have suggested that is what happened). Canseco is greedy, faithless, selfish, embittered, scornful, and everlastingly a showboat. He is a bad man, and that makes him retrospectively (except among those who claim to have felt this way always) a bad ballplayer. Not to mention a bad writer.

The question that concerns me in all this is not one of the obvious ones, like what to tell my children, or what to do about the problem of steroids, or how to think about the records that may have been broken by cheaters, or how to protect against perfidy, avarice, taint, and scandal the dear old national game. Like all obvious questions, none of these can be answered. All human endeavor is subject to cracking. It's the hard Tex Avery truth of the universe: Put your finger over one leak, and another one pops up just beyond your reach. Violence, gambling and game fixing, pestilential racism, overexpansion, competitive imbalance, labor strife, mindboggling cupidity, and cheating of every variety and school: For most of its history, the game of baseball, like everything we build, has been riddled with holes, some cavernous, some of them irreparable. I don't know what is to be done about the latest steroids debacle, and neither do you. No, what I want to know about Jose Canseco is: How come I still like the guy so much?

I'll go even further: I admire him. Not in the way I admire Clemente—not even remotely, which says something about what an ambiguous thing admiration can be. Like all showboats, Canseco courts the simpler kind of admiration, starting in the mirror each morning. He is slick, he drives too fast, he is nine feet tall and four feet wide and walks with a roosterish swagger. But there has always been something about him, about his style of play, his sense of self-mocking humor, his way of looking at you looking at him, that goes beyond vanity, self-aggrandizement, or being a world-class jerk-off.

Canseco has been described as a charmer and a clown, but in fact he is a rogue, a genuine one, and genuine rogues are rare, inside baseball and out. It's not enough to flout the law, to be a rogue—break promises, shirk responsibilities, cheat—you must also, at least some of the time, and with the same abandon, do your best, play by the rules, keep faith with your creditors and dependents, obey orders, throw out the runner at home plate with a dead strike from deep right field. Above all, you must do these things, as you do their opposites, for no particular reason, because you feel like it or do not, because nothing matters, and everything's a joke, and nobody knows anything, and most of all, as Rhett Butler once codified for rogues everywhere, because you do not give a damn. One day you make that breathtaking play at the plate from deep right. Another day you decide for no good reason to come into the game during the late innings of a laugher and pitch, retiring the side (despite allowing three earned runs on three walks and a pair of singles)—and forever ruining that cannon of an arm.

I've never seen a man who seems more comfortable than Jose Canseco with who he is—not with who we think he is, like George W. Bush, or with his best idea of himself, like Bush's predecessor, but with himself, charmer and snake, clown and thoroughbred. He doesn't care what you think of him; if anything, he derives a hair more pleasure from your scorn and contumely than he does from your useless admiration. By coming forward as he did to peel back the nasty bandage on baseball's wound, it was not that Canseco had nothing to lose, as some of his critics claimed. A man like Canseco never has anything to lose or to gain but his life and the pleasure he takes from it.

That this also remains exactly true for each of us is a thought that makes no impression on me in my daily intercourse with all of the things I give a damn about, and it probably makes none on you. We aren't wired to see things that way, and we can never be blockade runners, or Casablanca casino owners, or fatally gifted ballplayers who sometimes, as Canseco once did, permit a baseball to bounce off the top of our head before its departure from the ballpark. We have no style, you and I; only people who don't give a damn have style.

There was a time, though, when men like Canseco, without taking anything from the luster of men like Roberto Clemente, could also be accounted as heroes. They were the ones, the Ulysseses and Sinbads and Raleighs, who sailed to places we couldn't imagine, and then they returned, after a career of wonder, calamity, and chagrin, not one whit better than they were when they left. And surely no better than we—possibly worse. Yet in the end, they were the only ones fit to make the voyage, and when they came back, they carried a truth in their baggage that no one else would be clown enough, and rogue enough, and hero enough, to speak.

I Feel Good About My Murse

One of the fundamental axioms of masculine self-regard is that the tools and appurtenances of a man's life must be containable within the pockets of his jacket and pants. Wallet, keys, gum, show or ball game tickets, Kleenex, condoms, cell phone, maybe a lighter and a pack of cigarettes: Just cram it all in there, motherfucker. When I was a smoker—a long time ago—I used to predicate every purchase of a shirt, tee, or button-down on whether or not it featured a front pocket to hold my pack of Winston Lights. Take away everything, cigarettes, phone, even keys, a man remains a man so long as he keeps his wallet pressed up against his body. A wallet is a man's totem, his distillation. It pockets his soul as surely as he pockets it.

The necessary corollary to this inviolate principle is that no man, ever, ought to carry a purse. Purses are for women; a purse is basically a vagina with a strap. If you have diabetes, let's say, it is permitted to carry your works and your insulin around in a leather zip, but as soon as you start shoving your keys, Altoids, and above all your wallet in there, too, it's over. You are a man with a purse.

As firmly—as manfully—as I always adhered to this absolute prohibition, I suffered from its tyranny. I sat on my wallet (a behavior so harmful to the sciatic nerve that it can lead to a diagnosable syndrome called piriformis, or fat wallet syndrome), got raked repeatedly across the thigh by the mace of my keyring, bulged all over in unflattering ways like Wile E. Coyote after he swallows a live Roman candle. I was tormented by that household devil of every pocket, the Hole, an anarchic character whose satanic powers include the ability to cause you to forget its existence every time you put on the pants or the jacket it has chosen to haunt, right up to the moment that all ninety-six cents of your change go skittering and windchiming across the bus-station floor, or your Bic lighter slips down into the secret lining of your blazer.

Nevertheless, I adhered rigorously to the way of the pocket for the first few decades of my life as a would-be man. For years I wore a sport jacket wherever I went, no matter how unseasonable or inappropriate to the occasion, simply to take advantage of the additional pocket-space it afforded, a strategy whose reductio ad absurdum is the photojournalist vest, the kind they used to advertise in the old-school Banana Republic catalogs. There was a period during college and graduate school when I dragged around a knapsack, but even then I never relaxed my grip on manhood enough to carry anything other than books, pens, and maybe one of the elephantine Walkmans of that era, impossible to pocket—the only storage alternative was the dreaded belt clip,

a kind of prosthetic penis, in its own inverse way as emasculat-
ing as a purse.

Saggy-bottomed and stained from sitting around in puddles
of beer, the knapsack is—along with its sober older brother the
briefcase—one of a limited number of stealth purse strategies by
which men routinely attempt to circumvent, elude, or transcend
the cruel code of the pocket. The advent of the laptop computer
has led to a kind of renaissance in the category of luggage for-
merly occupied by the satchel, an all but forgotten item just a few
years ago, now more commonly designated a messenger bag and
hybridized in leather, nylon, and plastic, leading to all kinds of
knapsack-cum-attachés and tote-cum-briefcases. And there are
the gym bag, and the paratroop bag, and the flight bag, and those
other hopeful attempts to provide a man with a rugged GI Joe kind
of place to carry around his Walther PPK, his cyanide pills, his safe
cracking tools, and his Kiehl's lip balm. But check your pockets,
or the pockets of the man standing next to you, the one with the
commando kit–cum–road warrior carryall. I will bet you a cyanide
pill that he's still packing his wallet, keys, and spare change in
his pants. Otherwise, that rugged satchel becomes, by definition,
nothing but a purse.

It was the diaper bag that broke me. When my first child was
born, the idea that a bag intended for the transport of bottles,
ointment, nipples, and Huggies ought not to emasculate its male
bearer was a proposition only slightly more devoid of sense than
at the present time. Furthermore, it was not merely a feminine
aesthetic that guided the design of available diaper bags, but the

same bizarrely infantilizing principle that prevailed in maternity wear—bears and balloons and cheerily ersatz gingham—as if it were the baby herself and not her adult parents who would be schlepping the thing around. In the end I found a number in plain black nylon, disguised as a knapsack, with a zip-down changing pad. It still had the nipples and the ointment, but I hoped that in its blackness and angles, it might possess certain properties of stealth.

I carried that diaper bag until it became so saturated and coated with dairy and excretory residue that it needed to be disposed of by a hazmat team and a federal cleanup superfund. Three children followed the first, each with his or her diaper bag, and as fatigue, inattention, and habit took over, I stopped noticing if I was carrying the Esprit or the Kate Spade or the (forgive me) Petunia Pickle Bottom in embroidered lime-green Chinese silk. I had the diaper bag over one shoulder and a kid in the opposite arm, and I was pushing a stroller full of groceries, and some other small child was dragging along behind me hanging from the back pocket of my jeans, and at that instant as I left the store, I felt like it would be a lot easier just to drop my wallet into the diaper bag with my keys, and my cell phone, and my *New York Review of Books* than try to shove it down into my pants.

After that I got into the habit of carrying all my stuff around in the diaper bag. As my youngest kid got older and the need diminished for the full armamentarium—for the boxes of UHT milk, the Aquaphor, and the baby wipes—I broke down and bought a nice Jack Spade knapsack, black and slick, lined with sky blue. I tucked a couple of diapers and some wipes into it with my wallet and iPod and keys, and I set out.

But a knapsack is such a defeated thing, sitting there slumped and baggy-assed on the floor at one's feet. One sheds it wearily, with a beaten-down shrug of his shoulder. What's more, I was forty, and there was something at once preposterous and dismaying about returning after so many years to the accessory of my PBR and Nietzsche days. So I tried a satchel, a messenger bag, and a couple of those outsize hybrids thereof. But whatever themed adventure these bags attempted to suggest—soldier, spy, pierce-tongued tattooed bike messenger, laptop slacker—I felt like an impostor, a boy playing dress-up. I just wanted a bag that wasn't too big or too small or too heavy, one that would carry the things I needed—and inevitably some of the things my kids needed—without making me look too much like one of those Germano-Scandinavian tourists you see walking around New York in the summer with their zipper packs and clogs. I needed a purse. A man purse. A murse.

One day I was telling all this to a female friend of mine, an adventuresome shopper with a taste for the fabulous in men's clothing and a boyfriend who refused to wear anything but the most routine garb. She had already bestowed on me, because her man would not be caught dead in it, the gift of a silk multicolor-pinstriped Paul Smith muffler, and I could tell that the murse question piqued her interest; indeed, she seemed to take an almost philosophical interest in the problem.

"You don't want too mursy of a murse," she said. "You don't want to look like one of those Swedish guys."

"No."

"Next thing you'll be wearing clogs."

"God forbid."

"It has to be sort of masculine somehow, but not goofy. Not army surplus. Not Jamaican bike messenger."

"You echo my thoughts exactly."

"I mean, the thing is, it's a purse. You are going to be carrying a purse. I don't think you can really get around that or try to hide it. Nor should you."

"Nor do I wish to hide it," I said. "If people want to mock me or think less of me or just laugh their asses off when they see me walking around with a purse, I am prepared to face their scorn."

"Kind of like the Jackie Robinson of purse-wearing men," my friend said.

"Kind of just like that," I said.

There is nothing brave or courageous or remotely Robinson-esque about my contemplating the carrying of a purse, any more than there is in my taste for pink shirts, though I was once informed by a mother of my acquaintance, half disapprovingly, that wearing a pink shirt was a brave thing for a man to do. It's simply the case that as I get older, I seem every day to give a little bit less of a fuck what people think of or say about me. This is not the result of my undertaking to exercise a moral program or of increased wisdom or of any kind of willed act on my part. It just seems to be a process, a time-directed shedding, like the loss of hair or illusions. I am a husband, a father, and a son, whether or not I think, ponder, or worry about gender, sexuality, my life as a man;

and maybe there's a kind of pleasure to be taken in simple uncon-
sciousness, an automatic way of moving and being and acting in
the world. And maybe for an instant here and there, in the taking
of that pleasure, I partake of a grace like the grace of Jackie Robinson.

A week after I talked to my friend, a purse came UPS. It's a
square of fawn-colored suede, about the size of an extra-small
pizza box, trimmed in brown leather with white stitching. It has
a strap of cotton webbing, dark brown with a tan stripe running
down the center. It's handsome, soft and rugged at the same time
the way only suede can seem. And it's definitely a purse. It holds
my essential stuff, including a book—for true contentment, one
must carry a book at all times, and great books so rarely fit, my
friends, into one's pocket—but no more, and so I can wear it, and
my masculinity, and my contempt for those who might mock or
misunderstand me, very lightly indeed.

[VI]

ELEMENTS OF FIRE

Burning Women

The second burning woman was small and dark-haired, pert, buxom, younger than my mother but not as pretty. I had never seen her. As had her predecessor a few months earlier, she sat behind the wheel of her car, an orange AMC Matador parked with the engine off at the end of our driveway, windows rolled down. She sat staring with hollow shock at the Boyfriend's Mustang, which was in turn parked at the head of our driveway, under the basketball hoop mounted on the edge of the carport.

"Hello," I said, stooping to retrieve the Post.

"Hello," said the woman.

It was already hot, the sky cloudless, the air dense and starry with gnats, the sun well up over the trees.

"How are you this morning?" I said.

The woman eyed me skeptically as if I were a consolation prize or parting gift sent out by the Boyfriend, who was at that moment sitting at our kitchen table, eating a large bowl of oatmeal that I had made for him—slightly chunky, slightly chewy, and yet smooth and pleasantly glutinous, which I served with sultana raisins, a dissolving puddle of brown sugar, and a nice thick spiral of half-and-half. One of the ongoing puzzles I posed to myself at the age of fifteen was the gap between the things that I knew or felt and the things that I did. Such as, to cite one example, the lengths to which I would go to please the Boyfriend, whom I loathed, and yet whose rough-edged, racy laugh or few words of praise for my cooking could bring tears to my eyes.

"What's your name?" said the burning woman. She was actually quite pretty, sloe-eyed and freckled with a snub nose and breasts that registered strongly on my tricorder's bodacity detection array.

"Mike," I told her.

"Mike."

"Michael. It means 'Who is like unto God?' It's a question."

"Do you spell it with a question mark?"

"No, but maybe I should. That could be cool."

"Do me a favor, Mike?"

"Tell him that you were here?"

She rummaged a package of Eve cigarettes from her purse and pushed in the dashboard lighter. "Done this before," she said, "I gather."

"Yes. Not every day, but."

My mother was one of a number of attractive women in the city of Columbia, Maryland, who were collectively embarked upon the bold enterprise of having their hearts broken by the Boyfriend, whose movements were like those of a guerrilla leader or rebel commander, never sleeping in the same bed longer than two or three nights running. In the interests of security, the Boyfriend apparently thought nothing of dividing one night between two or more beds. The women who loved the Boyfriend tended, like my mother, to be strangely slow on the uptake when it came to grasping the bitter truth about the man, but once they realized that he had been lying to them and running around town with several other women at once, they tended to go through a period—relatively prolonged in my mother's case—of following him and tracking his movements. Come to think of it, very much like stealthy operatives of a conquering power bent on crushing insurrection. My mother had the Boyfriend that morning, but I knew that only two nights before, she had crept out of the house at two o'clock in the morning to go and stand in the bushes outside the house of another woman in whose driveway the Boyfriend's Mustang sat, engine clicking.

My mother was, and remains, a cool customer. Not cold, if by cold you mean unfeeling or remote, heartless, or disengaged. But not unduly given, let's say, to bursting into flame. Big shows of emotion, tears and drama, shouting, proclamations, bold naked statements of love and hate, braggadocio and stomping around—these are not the arts of her hardheaded, soft-spoken race. The woman is considered. Deliberate. Measured. Unflappable. Skeptical and sharp-eyed. Generous with her time and attention, unstinting with sound advice, and steady in her bestowal of moral support, she has never been your Santa Claus of physical affection with the lap and the cookies and the great big sack full of hugs. Hugs when she's happy, hugs when you're sad, hello, good-bye, lunch, breakfast, warm soft armloads of love for everyone: not she.

It was quite unexpected, therefore—the right word might be *freakish*—when my mother, slowly at first, almost imperceptibly, like a leaf that chances to blow into the bright focus of somebody's spectacles left out in the sun, set herself on fire for the Boyfriend. In the years since my parents' separation had become final, she'd dated a lot of men, a zoo's worth, furry and hairless as mole rats, a kitchen drawer's worth, sharpened and dull. Line them up and they varied in form, tint, and potency like bottles on the back of a bar. Some had been handsome, fit, deep-voiced, and deep-pocketed. Some had come around too much and given her too many rash presents, and others had been aloof and trifled with her time. Some had paid heed to me and my opinions, enough so that I minted fresh opinions for them at twice my usual rate. Others had felt it wisest to proceed to my mother's bedroom without taking note of the young man on the stairs, in the horned helmet, posing a pertinent question about runes.

In all that time until the Boyfriend, I never saw my mother fall in love, not even a little. And lest this seem a matter of perception or simple wishful thinking on the part of a son perhaps jealous of his mother's time and affection, looking to do what he could to drive away the likely candidates or downplay the intensity of his mother's feelings toward them, there was my mother's own testimony, repeated over the years with suitable variation, in con-versation with her girlfriends or to me alone on a drive somewhere far enough that the conversation had time, with my little brother snoring in the backseat, to turn to her love life: *He's nice enough. A little dull. I don't think this is really heading anywhere. If he calls, tell him I'm not in.*

The truth of the matter is that from the moment the very first suitor turned up—call him Roger, call him mustached and tweedy and festooned with an Isro—and I realized that such a thing was possible, I had been waiting for my mother to fall in love. It was something I wanted to see, something I knew was fully possible, and not just because I knew that even Vulcans went love-amok once every seven years and that, as our World Book encyclopedia informed me, under the ice of Iceland there burned fires of molten steel. No, I had seen proof of my mother's ardor in black and white. This photograph—take a look.

My mother and father in the summer of 1962 on a blanket in the sun. A grassy slope, a distant tree. My father, shirtless and smooth, holds my mother in his arms; he's lying right on top of her. Her head is thrown back to expose to his mouth her throat, and her bare shoulders are in a halter top. Her hand, fingers splayed, is pressed against the flesh of his back, keeping him, playing him, holding him there. The first time I came upon this picture tucked between the pages of my father's Modern Library edition of *The Poetry of Blake*, I was stunned, transfixed by this evidence that in some remote era there must have once existed, as some part of me had always known there must, a kingdom or a civilization or some kind of lost world known, to scholars of dust, as my parents' love for each other. It was like seeing at long last some kind of theory or explanation of myself, of how I got here, and almost literally so, for printed in the bottom border of the picture were the words AUGUST 1962, and it was not quite ten months later that there came into the world, squalling and shitting, the author of these lines. And that was the reason, I think, that I wanted to see my mother in love. Not because armed with this proof of their having once loved each other I hoped that in some whistle-while-you-wish *Wonderful World of Disney* way it would be my father toward whom she once again would kindle her heart, but because something made sense to me, looking at the picture, that had never made sense before. In the absence of the kind of passion, of fire, to which the photograph attested, what was the point of it all? Why else had they done it—built it all up so they could then knock it all down? After a marriage breaks, there is nothing more point-less than the child, to that child, of that marriage.

The lighter popped out, and the second burning woman looked into its radiant coils for a moment, then reached in and poked them with the tip of her finger. I could hear the hiss of her flesh as it singed. Actually, it was not that long since I had con-ducted the very same experiment with the lighter in our Impala, perhaps out of the same aimless and darkly curious urge. Would I be like her one day? Come to the same dire pass, driving around all night in the pursuit, at once brazen and furtive, of the thing that was hurting me the most? Fervently, I hoped and dreaded that it would be so.

"Ah!" she said. "Ouch." She held her cigarette to the heat, in-haling a savage puff to get it going, then shook out her fingers as if drying polish on her nails. Then she told me her name, which I no longer remember. "You can tell him I was here, Mike. All right?"

"Yes, ma'am."

"Miss."

"Yes, miss."

"And tell him I had fun last night chasing him all around town."

"Did you have fun?"

"Not a minute," said the burning woman, and then she drove off into the flames.

Verging

When I was fifteen, I slept with this woman I knew. I'm not sure how old she was at the time; probably not over thirty-five. She was a friend of my mother's, and I have never known, then or to this day, what was in it for her. I was a newly thin, undistinguished-looking kid with acne and aviator glasses. My long hair was cut and styled in the "wings" that render hilarious contemporary photographs of Shaun Cassidy and Leif Garrett. Though I was smart, verbal, and took an interest in the world around me—and had recently felt stirrings of some kind of new grasp on the nature of my life to come, derived from reading *The World According to Garp* and watching *Annie Hall*—that interest still quickened most keenly in proximity to things like *Dune*, Jim Starlin's *Warlock*, and the stories of H.P. Lovecraft. I have devoted many passing moments over the intervening years to observing interactions between thirty-five-year-old women and fifteen-year-old boys, and I have found that all the mystery in the business lies on the older and wiser side of things.

My mother threw a party, and there was dancing that ran late into the evening, with the tempos slowing as the night wore on until, in the end, my mother and her boyfriend went off someplace to do whatever they did, and I found myself alone in the arms of this woman—divorced, single, sweet-smelling—subject to her languid, teasing conversation, to the pressure of her belly against my hips, and to the tender mercies of Willie Nelson singing "Help Me Make It Through the Night."

Maybe the solution to all the mystery lies in the title and lyrics of that song—and in the ache of the voice that was singing it. I am certain the woman was pretty drunk.

"Are you a virgin?" she said in an offhand tone.

"No," I said. I was happy to see that my reply surprised her. It was the truth, and I was hoping it would be enough to persuade her to extend the invitation that I thought she might be contemplating.

"Does your mother know that?"

"Well, I didn't tell her," I said. "I don't think so."

"I don't think so, either," said my mother's friend.

My virginity had been no particular encumbrance to me, and it had not lingered very long beyond the time that I started hankering to be rid of it. I was in the tenth grade, a year younger than most of my fellow sophomores, and the girl who had done me the favor was a senior: a sophisticate of seventeen, in possession of a keen mind and a tremendous American automobile of the period (an LTD? an Olds '88?) that she used to drive herself responsibly to museums, film retrospectives, and concerts. She was a serious reader (I still have her paperback copy of *The Wreckage of Agathon*, and I plan to read it someday), a musician, an artist; an incipient adult, embarked on a history of unfolding adventure, both intellectual and physical, in which I was to rate barely a footnote. Her long-term steady boyfriend, to whose own brilliant incipience, as I was all too aware, I offered nothing in the way of competition, had left for college earlier in the fall with an exchange of vague promises of fidelity. She may have been lonely, missing him, looking for ways to strike back or strike out on her own. I didn't care in the least. He was the first ex-boyfriend whose shade was ever invoked in the memories and pillow talk of a girl I was fucking, and just as great a fool as all who followed him.

She was not much to look at—raw-cheeked, long-nosed, tall, and deceivingly prim—but that was okay with me. She had as much to forgive as I did, and in any case, I have never found anything more reliably sexy in a woman than a passion for 1) reading difficult novels and 2) me. We had been selected by the casting director of destiny to play Mr. and Mrs. Antrobus in the school production of *The Skin of Our Teeth*, and in time-honored Dick-and-Liz fashion, one thing led to another. I got her to laugh at something I said, and then she passed me a note in the hallway, ornamented with a star of glitter and glue. After the elapse of a gratifyingly brief interval she brought me home to her bedroom in the basement of her family's town house, and she bestowed upon me the magic of her permission.

I will try as hard as I can not to exaggerate here: I estimate that I spent merely forty-three minutes of the prolonged episode that followed in conducting a detailed and glorious survey, a USGS mapping expedition, complete with aerial reconnaissance and depth soundings, of the young woman's vagina. I would not affirm that I was more interested in studying it than in introducing my penis therein, but it was awfully close. I had spent years looking at doubtful (and in the end worthless) photographs of vaginas in scrounged copies of *Penthouse* and *Hustler*. In the end these proved to bear as much relation to the wonder of which I found myself that night—the unchallenged and loving custodian—as the portrait of a daube of beef in a cookbook bears to the fragrant, homely, hard-earned stew that presents itself, steaming on a plate, to the nose and eyes of a hungry man.

That was a Saturday night; the next day my mother took my brother and me out to Falls Church, Virginia, to visit our grandmother. I had not showered or washed my hands, and I spent the whole day dreaming over the smell of her on my fingers. I was a traveler returned from a fabled land. I wanted to tell everyone—my brother, my mother, my grandmother—what splendors and vistas I had encountered. The next weekend there was a dance, and my first lover invited me afterward into the great dark wastes of her backseat, where there was no time for science or exploration. And then on Monday she dumped me.

She had done me so many favors—had indulged, with a tenderness that even at the time I recognized as a kind of grace, all my exclamations over and examinations of her body, especially that astonishing evolutionary feat of origami between her legs—and now she did me the final one of being honest. She liked me, she said, and she liked having sex with me, but I was too young for her. I would not talk to her in the hallways of school when my male friends were around; I would not hold hands or hang out on the blacktop or in the cafeteria. In short, I was not comfortable with all the essential ancillaries of having a girlfriend. I could not handle it. I was—somehow she said it without hurting my feelings or inspiring any kind of attempt at denial from me—too immature.

No such compunction or misgiving seemed to trouble my mother's friend. As in a letter to *Penthouse* Forum, my mother and brother conveniently left town on the weekend following the late-night party, and I was by myself. My second lover came over around nine that Saturday night, much later than I would have liked, since by the time she arrived, looking pretty and smelling very good and carrying an impossibly adult bottle of wine, I was already wishing, with a fervor that shocked me, to get the whole thing over with.

I led her into the living room, and we sat down on two chairs. I managed to get the wine open, and she drank a little, and I pretended to drink a little, and then with the quenching heat of the wine against my dry throat, I took a long dark swallow. *Here I am,* I thought, *pretending to care for wine, pretending to speak wittily of inconsequential things, pretending to be the kind of kid whose mother's girlfriends decide to come over and throw him a fuck.* I guess at some point we must have started to make out. I employed the careful, phased techniques, starting at the top of one's partner and working ritualistically down, that I had been taught by my seventeen-year-old ex-non-girlfriend.

"We don't need to do all that teenager stuff," said my mother's friend. "Where should we go?"

I suggested that we do it right there on the floor, on the green-

and-blue shag rug, and that was what we did. When it was over, I rolled off and instructed her, in very plain terms, to go home. I felt none of the rapture, the stunned cartographic joy I had felt during and after my first time. Though objectively, she was much better-looking—soft and shapely—I had no desire to make a study of her. I had wanted to get the thing over with, and so I had.

"Go?" she said, and I saw to my horror that I had hurt her feelings. "But I—"

I actually employed the words "I just remembered that I have an appointment," which is how I know for sure that I was fifteen. "I have to go see a friend."

"Oh," she said, and her eyes resumed their customary sly-eyed coolness. "Okay."

She sat up and pulled on her underpants, rolled her tights back up her white thighs, shivered herself into her wool jumper. I wanted to tell her, to explain to her, that I was not ready, that I was too immature, that I just couldn't handle it. She stood up and gathered her purse and her coat, and I saw her to the door, where she turned to me, her eyes looking vulnerable again, wondering, maybe asking me to help her make it through the night. And suddenly, with the smell of wine and cunt in the air between us, I wanted to do it again, in a bed, all night and with science and art.

"Good night," she said. She kissed me in a final kind of way. I stood on the doorstep until she got into her car, started the engine, and drove home, leaving me one regret, one empty house, one night closer to being ready.

Fever

I was standing on Forbes Avenue, across from the laboratory where I had sold my blood plasma to buy irises and halvah for Rebecca, the first great love of my life, waiting for the bus that would take me to her lover's house. It was one o'clock in the morning. Giddy fireworks of snow exploded over my head in the light from the streetlamp; there were already four inches on the ground. Under my peacoat I wore only a pajama top, and in my haste to get out the door, I'd neglected to put on my overshoes. My gloves I had lost weeks before. I carried my frozen hands in my pockets, the right one jammed in beside a dented Grove Press edition of *Illuminations*, Rebecca's favorite book, which, like Rebecca herself, couched everything in terms of torment and ecstasy and moved me strangely without making much sense.

"This is very embarrassing, Mike," Rebecca's lover had said over the phone. "But I'm just incredibly fucked up, and I think there might really be something wrong with her. She keeps making this sound." Alarmed, half asleep, I'd told him I would be there as soon as I could. An hour spent waiting for the 61C, sneakers ankle-deep in a pool of black slush, had given me ample time to wonder why, given the circumstances, I should be the one to rescue Rebecca yet again from the burning-down house of her brain. Let him, the other man, begin to lose nights of his life in emergency rooms and in the lyrical labyrinths of her mysterious fevers and furors.

My anger abated somewhat in the warmth of the bus's interior and by well past two, when I reached the Squirrel Hill duplex where Rebecca's lover lived, I had once more donned the full panoply, the ax, tackle, and stouthearted gravity, of a resolute fireman of love. I would save Rebecca if it was not already too late. When her lover opened the door, I thought he was going to tell me that she had died.

"She's upstairs," he said. He was willowy, frail, with the smooth cheeks and puffy eyes of a newborn. Like Rebecca, he admired aesthetic suicides and madmen such as van Gogh and Syd Barrett. His health was poor, he wore heavy wool sweaters even in the heat of August, and to counteract the jitters of a stomach so nervous that he threw up just waiting for a DJ to play his request on the radio, he smoked great quantities of marijuana. We had not seen each other since the night two weeks earlier when I learned that he was Rebecca's lover. I wanted him to look mortified now, chastened by my gallant fireman's air, but he seemed only stoned and not much put out. He shied away from the blast of cold wind that had followed me like a pack of dogs into the house. "Man, I don't know what happened to her. She just kind of fell over."

"Michael?" Rebecca called as I came up the stairs. The house had the old-potato stink of bong water, and the steam heat was turned all the way up. There was a childish note of shame in her voice, and as I came into the sweltering bedroom of her lover and caught her smell of lily of the valley, I felt my heart, like a muscular reflex or spasm, forgive her. "Michael, what are you doing? I'm all right."

Her forehead was damp, her eyes clouded with fever tears. I stood up. I looked at her lover's bed. There were shoes in the bedsheets, a Coke bottle, an open jar of cold cream, plates streaked with hardened food. On the nightstand they had built a tiny Stonehenge of pill bottles and bronchial inhalers, and on one slipless pillow sat a porcelain water pipe in the shape of a human skull.

"We're going home," I told her. "Come on."

"Please, Michael." She looked at her lover reproachfully, I thought. "I don't want to go outside."

Couldn't she see that the house all around her was falling in a shower of sparks and burned beams? Ignoring Rebecca's protests, I helped her down the stairs, zipped her into her parka, pulled on her red rubber boots, tucked her piano-black hair into her knit beret. I called a taxi that took us back to the apartment on Meyran Avenue, and I gave my last five dollars to the driver. I put her in bed, and told her I loved her, and tried to enfold all her trembling limbs in the warm envelope of my body.

Rebecca moved out two days later and ever since, as far as I know, has been leaping, afire, from high windows that belch black smoke. In all that time, though there have been many other leapers, I have never managed to catch a single one, or learned how to stand back and just watch them fall.

Looking for Trouble

One spring afternoon when I was fifteen years old, a kid who was new to the tenth grade showed up at our front door unannounced, with a backgammon set folded under his arm. I had no talent for backgammon or friend-making. I hated games that, like backgammon or the making of friends, depended in any way on a roll of the dice or a gift for seizing opportunities. I disliked surprises and all changes of plan, even changes for the better—except in retrospect. At the art of retrospection I was a young grandmaster. (If only there were a game whose winning required a gift for the identification of missed opportunities and of things lost and irrecoverable, a knack for the belated recognition of truths, for the exploitation of chances in imagination after it is too late!) True, I might have felt some disposition to like this kid already, but I never would have dared to act upon it. I was an early subscriber to Marxian doctrine as espoused by Woody Allen in *Annie Hall*, which had been my favorite movie for the last year or so, and the mere fact that this kid wanted to be friends with me at all seemed to impeach his judgment and fitness for the role.

"I thought you seemed like someone who might enjoy back-gammon," said the kid, gravely mistaken.

I stood there at the front door with nothing in particular to do—I think I was reading a book when he knocked, likely some book I had already read—no good friend my age to speak of, no plausible excuse to send him away, though every strand and dendrite of instinct crying out to be left alone to my friendless but well-planned solitude. I think I might have told him that I had homework, or I had to take care of my little brother, or since my mother was at work, we weren't allowed to have anybody over. I might have tried to be honestly rude and said that I had no interest in backgammon at all. But the confirmed stick-in-the-mud will always fall victim to the interventions of other people acting on impulse, because if habit is his religion, then his Satan is change, and in the end, we are all prey to temptation.

I said he might as well come in, and he wiped the floor with me several times at backgammon until I confessed—armed with fresh evidence—that I hated the game, and we found something else to do. Within a few weeks he had become the best friend, save one, that I have ever had.

In 1992, almost exactly fifteen years after that afternoon, this kid, grown now to a man, called to tell me about this girl, woman, whatever. She shared a Stuyvesant Town apartment on the Lower East Side with his friend Audrey, and she had just been dumped by her boyfriend, among whose numerous flaws, apart from the chief flaw of not appreciating her, were a staunch Catholicism and a lack of Catholicism when it came to practicing a certain act of oral love-making extremely popular among many women who have tried it.

"I told her I knew a Jewish guy who would give her head," my friend explained, kidding, not kidding at all. He assured me that the young woman in question was smart, attractive, lively, fun to be around. He had taken her out himself once. Though they liked each other, there was no spark.

"A blind date," I summarized in a doubtful if not faintly nauseated tone when he had finished unfolding the backgammon set of his proposition.

At this epoch, after a period of adventure and modest uproar, my life had resumed, like Larry Talbot after a lycanthropic spree, its true shape: a dull business. I was living in a small carriage-house apartment in the Hudson Valley, two hours north of the city, in the fifth year of trying to finish my second novel: alone with a book again. Nothing to do, nobody to do it with, nothing going on at all. Just the way I liked it, or rather, just the way I always seemed to fall out, whether I did like it that way or not. When it came to the art of living, the only medium susceptible to my genius was inertia. If someone wanted to get married, I would marry her. If she wanted out, then it was time to get a divorce. Otherwise, in either case, I was okay with things the way they were. No, not okay: I longed and suffered and pined with the rest of humanity. Sometimes I was happy enough with the book I was reading or the book I was writing, and the life I was stuck inside felt like a house on a rainy day. But most of the time I was just plain dying to get out. All

I needed—all I have ever needed—was someone to challenge me, to serve as a goad, an instigator, a stirrer of the pot. I hated trouble, but I loved troublemakers. I hated chance and uncertainty, but I was drawn to those who showed up on your doorstep with their own pair of dice.

"Suit yourself," said my old friend when I declined this girl's number. He was getting ready to hang up on me and my dial tone of a life.

I could feel the familiar sensation as I said goodbye to him, the train pulling away from the platform, the call to adventure fading on the air, the tumult in the blood as the moon tries to fight its way out from behind a cloud and turn a man to a wolfman. Longing for change and fearing it, caught in a tissue woven from dread and regret shot through with purest gold threads of a yearning to get out of my book, my room, my house, my body, my skull, my life.

"All right," I said, as I had said to him when he bicycled over with his backgammon board. "Just give me her number."

Not very long afterward, in an ongoing act of surrender to the world beyond my window, with no possibility of knowing what joy or disaster might result, I married her. And since that afternoon in Berkeley, California, standing along the deepest seam of the Hayward Fault—no, since our first date—this woman has dragged, nudged, coaxed, led, stirred, embroiled, mocked, seduced, finagled, or carried me into every last instance of delight or sorrow, every debacle, every success, every brilliant call, and every terrible mistake, that I have known or made. I'm grateful for that, because if it were not for her, I would never go anywhere, never see anything, never meet anyone. It's too much bother. It's dangerous, hard work, or expensive. I lost my ticket. I kind of have a headache. They don't speak English there, it's too far away, they're closed for the day, they're full, they said we can't, it's too much bother with children along.

She will have none of that. She is quick, mercurial, intemperate. She has a big mouth, a rash heart, a generous nature (always a liability, in my view), and if my way is always to opt out, to sit in the window seat with a book in my lap, pressing my face against the pane, then her great weakness, indistinguishable from her great strength, is a fatal, manic aptitude for saying yes. She gets herself, and us, and me, into trouble: into noble causes and silly disputes, into pregnancies and terminations, into journeys and strange hotel beds and awkward situations, into putting my money where my mouth is and my name on fund-raising pitch letters for the things that I believe in but otherwise, I don't know, haven't gotten around to yet. She is the curse and the wolfman charm in my blood, calling me to shed my flannel shirt and my pressed pants with their sensible belt and lope on all fours into the forest.

Once she and I found ourselves talking about this picture that hangs on the wall of our house. It's a magnificent Lothar Osterburg photogravure, shadowy and mysterious, of a miniature clipper sailing across a scale-model ocean. This picture seemed to both of us to embody our marriage—I was the sails, and she was the tiller. Or vice versa. Honestly, I can't quite remember how it seemed at the time. But I know that in considering the image of that great ship in full sail, what we both understood, have always understood, was that whether I am the wind and she is the waves, or she is the rigging and I am the rudder—at this point I have pretty much exhausted my nautical vocabulary—the crucial point for a moral landlubber like me is that we are embarked. I answered the call of adventure; I rolled the dice. I jumped out of the window, holding tightly to her hand. See us, sailing into the blue.

A Woman of Valor

When I was nine years old, I fell in love with a super-heroine whose unlikely name—a name that still brings me a wince of lust and embarrassment when I say it—was Barda. Big Barda. I have never recovered, thank God, from my first sight of her in *Mister Miracle* #8 (September 1972).

The intricate pop-Zoroastrian theology of the comic books that Jack Kirby drew at DC Comics in the early seventies (in which Mister Miracle, "Super Escape Artist," figured prominently) is wonderful, nutty, and hard to summarize. For now I'll just say that Big Barda, commander of the Female Fury Battalion, was born and reared for a life of perpetual combat on a world called Apokolips by a Dickensian harridan with the cruel-irony name of Granny Goodness. Barda dressed in elaborate armor of dark blue scale mail with a vaguely pharaonic battle helmet, and she carried a fearsome chunk of hardware (admittedly somewhat ambiguous from the Freudian point of view) called a Mega-Rod. As for her eponymous immensity, it was not merely physical; everything she did partook of the bigness that was the essence of her character. She spoke in exclamations and displayed Rabelaisian appetites for food and drink. She was brusque, sardonic, hot-tempered, and did not endure patiently the doubts and tergiversations of anyone less intelligent or quick to seize the moment than herself. And to my knowledge, she was the first superheroine in the history of comic books whose personal courage, moral integrity, and astute intelligence, though they pervaded all her actions, were most joyfully expressed through her willingness, when necessary, to kick ass.

Say *superheroine* and most people, I suppose, will think of Wonder Woman. With the possible exception of Supergirl, she is certainly the best known, or maybe it would be more accurate to say the most recognizable of costumed comic-book females. Wonder Woman is strong, and buxom and noble-intentioned, and when necessary she, too, has never hesitated to knock some heads together. When I was a boy, she was, as she remains to this day (because of her ancillary trademark value as a superficially feminist icon), a star in the firmament of DC Comics, far more important than Big Barda could ever hope to be.

Now, I have heard some women say over the years that growing up they liked Wonder Woman (an affection that says less about the character, I think, than about the thirst and adaptability of young girls seeking female heroes in the relative desert of comic books).

But she never came anywhere near reconfiguring, like Barda did, the erotic topography of my brain.*

Wonder Woman's story just never added up. It made no narrative sense. Her motivation, her purpose in life, her relations to men and their world had been formulated and reformulated by a succession of writers over the years without ever growing any clearer. We were told that she was an Amazon princess of misty origin, a demigoddess, heiress to Hellenic splendor and daughter of Queen Hippolyta herself, and yet she dressed in a costume that appeared to have been aired previously by a burlesque dancer at the Gayety in Baltimore, Maryland, on the Fourth of July 1933. I learned from my reading of Jules Feiffer's seminal *The Great Comic Book Heroes* that the early stories, which I read in cheap reprints, had been accused of promoting low morals, and I had noticed that they did seem to feature a lot of scenes of Wonder Woman tying people up or being tied up herself. But at the age of nine, I didn't get what *that* was all about. I still don't, come to think of it. At any rate, Wonder Woman had abandoned bondage and domination nearly a quarter of a century before, her magic golden lasso of compulsion the only surviving trace of those wild days.

This lasso formed one third of Wonder Woman's essential toolkit, along with her bullet-scattering bracelets and her invisible airplane. What any of these had to do with Greek mythology, "The Star-Spangled Banner," or one another, only the late Dr. William

---

* Of course, Lynda Carter as Wonder Woman (ABC 1975–76, CBS 1977–79) is another matter entirely.

Moulton Marston, her creator, knew for sure. A *lasso!* An invisible *airplane!* Even her secret identity, Diana Prince, felt gratuitous, un-lived—she might have abandoned it at any time without cost to anyone, least of all herself. Rooted in mythology, Wonder Woman never generated any mythology of her own; she contradicted her-self without struggling against or embodying those contradic-tions; in other words, she had no story. Only a narrative—only a woman with a narrative—can truly engage the erotic imagina-tion. Everyone else is just a pinup.

Supergirl, then. She was Superman's cousin, it may be re-called, Kara El, born and raised in Argo City on the planet Kryp-ton. She was a blonde, well constructed (all superheroines must be well constructed). Always a tad on the perky side, to my way of thinking. She looked nothing like her older cousin; what she looked like was the classic shiksa as envisioned by Jewish men of the day. She had all the classic shiksa accoutrements: a Super-Cat, a Super-Horse, a girlish Super-Room of her own. She hung out with the clean-cut, earnest teenagers of the future—they came from all over the galaxy, and yet they were all goyim—at the thirtieth-century headquarters of the Legion of Superheroes. She wore, one sensed, a formidable brassiere. But Supergirl had more soul than Wonder Woman. It was a sisterly, Laurie Partridge brand of soul: chipper, maybe, but tinged with parental loss. She had the tragic Superman streak, the central existential knowledge that her mighty powers derived from her greatest sorrow.

At the same time, Supergirl constituted a betrayal of one of the key elements of the Superman myth—that he was the sole survivor of a destroyed world, the eternal orphan. Inevitably, perky and ample as she might be, Supergirl cheapened the drama of Superman. She gave off a whiff of exploitation, of endless writers seeking endless variations on a theme. She had the elements of a narrative, but it was largely a borrowed one, an echo of that of her superfamous cousin. She did not possess her own mythology so much as belong to Superman's, right along with Krypto, and the Phantom Zone, and Bizarro, and the City of Kandor in its bottle. She was, finally, ancillary, inferior, a kid. She was not Superwoman—there was apparently no room for a Superwoman. She was all-powerful, yet she did not command.

Across town and in another universe, at Marvel, the pickings were, to be honest, probably worse. It took Marvel Comics years to begin to put together any worthwhile superheroines. To a gal, the first crop was embarrassingly disappointing. They had all the measly powers that fifties and sixties male chauvinism could contrive to bestow on a superwoman. For example, one of these ladies could make herself very, very small. Another could render herself invisible whenever she chose. Several employed witchery or some enhanced form of women's intuition. One was the black widow type and knew karate. And so on. It was not until a character called the Valkyrie came along in the seventies that a Marvel Comics heroine established herself as entirely her own woman, no one's wife or sister or daughter or girlfriend, no one's archenemy-ess. The Valkryie's winged horse, Aragorn, you suspected, would have wiped the floor with Supergirl's fussy, effeminate Comet. A few years after the Valkyrie, a sword-swinging, fiery barbarian named Red Sonja came along, brought to more vivid life than any preceding superheroine by artist Frank Thorne during a glorious eleven-issue run. As I look back, I see that the 1970s were a pretty good time for Amazons.

I guess it was inevitable that comic book writers and artists, looking for source material, would turn now and then to the Amazon. That was the archetype underlying the very first superheroine (though come to think of it, Wonder Woman's problem all along was that she never lived up to her Amazon billing), and from time to time in the history of comics—though not very often—independent, freebooting heroines like Sheena the Queen of the Jungle popped up: tough and strong but, more important, beholden to no one. Sheena, the Valkyrie, and Red Sonja were unencumbered by any glasses-wearing, steno-pad-carrying secret identity. There was no unwitting, patronizing lunk of a boyfriend or super-date, no repressive cover story to get tangled in. They did not shy from a fight—on the contrary, they relished conflict. And they demanded to be treated as equals, to whatever extent their mostly male writers and artists were willing to grant. As fond as I may be of this type of character, I'm obliged to concede that the Warrior Woman is, in its way, as sexist a cliché as Shrinking Violet (tininess) or Phantom Girl (insubstantiality) or Light Lass (rendering any substance to the condition of *fluff*).

This is where Big Barda comes in.

Jack Kirby (born Jacob Kurtzberg in New York City in 1917) was a bit of a madman, a cultural magpie, self-taught, movie-crazy. He grew up scrapping on the Lower East Side. He had seen tough service under Patton. The harshness of the world and the wonder of the movies mingled freely in the comics that he drew. As he got older, his vision turned darker and darker, and his sense of the indifference of a hostile universe to human fortune increased. More and more in his work at Marvel during the late sixties, vast primal forces of Good and Evil fought a perpetual war to whose combatants our earth was at most a bystander, at worst a worthless speck of dust. This endless warfare, this broken universe, left a heavy mark in Kirby's work on human beings. It took strong people to stand up to it. Kirby's people grew more and more massive, statuesque. They strode across the panels like tragic Shakespearian giants, beset all around by men and creation, crackling with energy bolts. When they slammed into walls and buildings, the walls and buildings fell down. It was out of this late-Kirby world of grandeur and conflict and sorrow over the brokenness of the world that Big Barda came, brandishing her Mega-Rod.

Barda was up to the fight—any fight and then some. The world of fire that she was born into and the way she was raised had obliged her to learn to be strong, vigilant, resourceful, and submissive to no one. But her intelligence told her that conflict is a waste, of life and time and energy, and she regretted it. She had her own narrative—a history of sorrow, hardship, and achievement—and though it constituted only one part of the larger mythology of Kirby's epic, it was her part; she had earned it. She saw the wrongness, the wickedness, the unreasoning cruelty of the world, and though she had been trained to withstand it, her heart rebelled. Mighty, she used her strength and risked her freedom to help the weak. In time she would mutiny against the might-makes-right strictures of her home and attempt to form a partnership of physical and intellectual equals—with Mister Miracle, her paramour, the love of her life. In his company, in rare moments of quiet, she doffed her armor, laid down her Mega-Rod, and made him a gift—both of them knowing full well its value—of her vulnerability, her sorrow, the pain of her childhood and youth. She was a Valkyrie with a brain and an aching heart.

Kirby biographers and scholars generally agree that in her substantiality, Big Barda was modeled on a nude spread in *Playboy* of the actress Lainie Kazan; but in her substance, on the late Rosalind Kirby (née Goldberg), Jack's wife of fifty years.

This brings me to the real subject, or object, of these ruminations. After discovering Big Barda, I could never be happy with the run-of-the-mill heroines I encountered in my life, whether they were Amazons or Violets or wasps or invisible girls. Then one night I met this woman who was not—not at all—Big. Five feet tall, she generally went about unarmed. She had been raised not in the suicide slums and battle orphanages of Apokolips but on the maple-lined streets of Ridgewood, New Jersey. It was tough on her; she had been encouraged, like most girls at the time, to learn to shrink, to be witchy, to turn herself invisible. She was pretty much the proverbial slip of a girl—a size zero—but she had, I saw at once, an inner Bigness. Like Barda, she did not suffer fools gladly. She did not carry a Mega-Rod; she didn't need one. She had plenty of narrative; sometimes it seemed that she was *all* narrative, stories and incidents and catastrophes and triumphs, like

Churchill's definition of history, one damn thing after another. From time to time the frenzy of battle came upon her, and then the walls and buildings started to rock and crumble. In short, I had never met anyone more fit to command the Female Fury Battalion. Now that passing time, hard-earned wisdom, four pregnancies, and I have all conspired to free her from the cruel-irony dietary and body-image regimes of the Apokolips in which we raise our young women, I think she would fill out pretty nicely, given the opportunity, whatever mad armor Jack Kirby could dream up.

It's traditional in Jewish homes on the Sabbath for a husband to chant the poem called *Eshes Chayil*, "A Woman of Valor." In ancient biblical language, he praises her, articulating a litany of true womanly virtues: strength of body and mind, compassion, resourcefulness, reliability, artfulness. He praises her costume and her readiness for righteous battle. "She girds her loins in strength," he says, "and makes her arms strong." Every week, in every home—traditionally—every husband affirms this central truth to every wife: that she is, as that great Jewish mythographer Jack Kirby understood, his Big Barda. Alas, the chanting of this poem is not, I'm sorry to report, a tradition that my wife and I observe. These words will have to serve instead.

[VII]

PATTERNS OF EARLY ENCHANTMENT

Like, Cosmic

I recently read in a news report that *Voyager 2* is about to pass through our sun's termination shock. I'm not sure what that means—something to do with the limits of the solar wind and the entry into the interstellar medium that fills the space between stars—but it struck me because I've been thinking a lot about the two *Voyager* probes. I happened to listen to a podcast of WNYC's wonderful *Radiolab* program not long ago, an episode devoted to contemplating the romance and the grim realities of space travel. Into the latter category *Radiolab*'s hosts, Jad Abumrad and Robert Krulwich, placed impossible distances, unbearable extremes of temperature, implacable laws of gravity and time, and the likely rarity and fragility of spacefaring civilizations. To supply the romance, they presented a woman named Ann Druyan. She had been one of the members of the team that NASA recruited back in the mid-seventies to assemble the sounds and images encoded on the famous Golden Record that was carried on board *Voyager 1* and *Voyager 2* as a greeting to the galaxy and (necessarily, given the relatively slow pace of travel) as a message to the future. You know the one: whale songs, Brandenburg concertos and didgeridoo, thunder and rain, human heartbeats, and the synaptic crackle of an EEG. Druyan described how the shared sense of intimate grandeur and the freewheeling spirit she experienced while working to produce the Golden Record encouraged her to fall in love with, and eventually marry, one of her colleagues on the project. She revealed that the brain-function and circulatory sounds of a human being featured on the golden disc that NASA sent out into the endless emptiness, now traveling at a rate of 38,000 miles per hour toward the far-flung neighborhoods of the stars AC+79 3888 and Ross 248, were those of her own living body. They were recorded, she told Radiolab, more or less on the day she discovered she had fallen utterly and helplessly and giddily in love with that colleague, the project's originator, Dr. Carl Sagan. Her heart and brain; their efflorescing love; and the greetings of an entire planet lobbed with the glee of a paperboy across a trillion miles of space that may be home to no one at all.

Dr. Sagan appears to have been a bit of a pothead, and some have looked at the vast, brilliant, loopy, complicatedly simple interstellar communication schemes he adumbrated during the late sixties and seventies and concluded that marijuana must have been part of the impetus behind them. Intuitively, I feel both the merit and the injustice in this conclusion, for, like the grand schemes of Dr. Carl Sagan, I am myself a child of the 1970s. Toward the end of the summer of 1977, when in turn two Titan III rockets lifted *Voyagers* 1 and 2 into orbit and sent them on their arcing slingshot courses across the solar system, I was fourteen years old, and my favorite item of clothing was a T-shirt purchased on the boardwalk at Ocean City, Maryland, that depicted a square-rigged galleon in full sail across a sea of space out of whose misty distance there emerged the supernova eyes and nebular bosom of an intergalactic babe. My favorite novel was *Ringworld* (1970) by Larry Niven, in which a genetically lucky female flower child and a youth-drug-addicted, world-tripping old man become lovers and uncover (among other secrets) the hidden history of humankind while exploring a ring-shaped artificial "planet" a million miles in diameter. My favorite comic book was Jim Starlin's *Warlock* (1975–6), whose hero was a star-faring, all-powerful, golden-skinned loser trapped in a mutually self-destructive yet strangely empowering relationship with a vampiric gem embedded in his own forehead. It would be another few years before I got involved with marijuana, but when I did, all that I ever found, in a way, was more of what I had already known: that everything, if you stopped to think about it, was, like, cosmic, even—if not especially—the power of sex and love.

There is no more useless activity than that of periodization, the packaging of history, in particular cultural history, into discrete eras—the Jazz Age, the Greatest Generation, the Eisenhower years, the Sixties. Such periods can never be honestly articulated without recourse to so many demurrals and arbitrary demarcations, and the granting of so many exceptions, as to render them practically useless for any kind of serious historical purpose. In times of supposed license, repression reigns freely all around; in eras renowned for their conventionality, oddballs and freaks hoist their banners high. And yet when I heard the gifted and intelligent Ann Druyan wondering, fervently but not without a sense of her own goofiness, if perhaps ages hence some technomagical future alien race might be able to reconstitute, from the record of her brain waves, her feeling of incipient passion for her man and for the work they undertook together, as equals, partners, and lovers—to re-create the sense of how it felt to be Ann Druyan on an afternoon in New York City during those infatuated, boundary-breaking, termination-shock-crossing years—I knew that I was listening, carried as by a lonely probe across the distances, to the voice of the 1970s.

If we are conducting our lives in the usual fashion, each of us serves as a constant source of embarrassment to his or her future self, and by the same formula, all "eras" can be made to look ridiculous in retrospect. But the seventies have always been prone to more ridicule than their twentieth century cousin-decades, without anyone giving sufficient notice to the fact that it was the seventies themselves that originated the teasing (*Annie Hall*, *Nashville*, the Me Decade, "You're So Vain"). It required no retrospection for the occupants of the zone now understood as the seventies to acknowledge the goofiness in all their pieties and solipsisms, and it is a mark of our own naïveté (at least) to suppose that a straight-faced young tax attorney going out on a Saturday night in 1974 wearing platform boots, glitter mascara, and his hair combed up into a two-foot Isro, for example, did not realize that he looked pretty silly. It's just that looking like a fool was correctly understood to be a likely if not an inevitable result of the taking of risks.

The sense of liberation that resulted from such risk-taking, how-ever conventionalized or routine it became, was felt for a little while to be well worth the price in foolishness. We are crippled in so many ways today by the desire to avoid fashion mistakes, to elude ridicule—a desire that leads at one extreme to the smil-ing elisions of political candidates and on the other to the awful tyranny of cool—that this willingness to be foolish is hard for us to sympathize with or understand. In this age of Gawker.com, we have forgotten the seventies spirit of mockery that smirks at the pretensions and fatuities of others in a way that originates with and encompasses ourselves. Atom for atom, we are made of ex-actly the same stuff as all the stars and galaxies. That is one of the cosmic, *Warlock*-worthy facts that I learned in the seventies. If you drop the S in cosmic, you arrive at the understanding that vanity, pomposity, and foolishness are at once communal and individual, like stardust. And so are our aspirations and our longing, some-how, to survive. The personal is political was a mantra of seven-ties feminism, but the spirit of that age, embodied perfectly in the interstellar voyage of Ann Druyan's amorous EEG, might be more accurately summarized as The personal is universal, or The per-sonal is fucking cosmic, baby!

We tend, through films, novels, and television programs, to view the seventies as the decade when the wheels came off the cart, when, to quote an anthem of the time, "Girls will be boys and boys will be girls," when America fell from her pedestal of God-fearing rectitude or was replaced gradually by an Imagineered simulacrum of itself, when moms wore kaftans and dads wore huge sideburns and they both did Quaaludes and went to key parties, when the comforting if rigid old Puritan-Victorian rules of social conduct, shaken in the sixties, finally gave way altogether like a mudslide in a California canyon, when New York City tottered like a bellwether toward the apocalypse, and the blockbuster-film mentality that has spread and cheapened pretty much everything was born. Or else—as on *That 70s Show*—we view the time, compared to the present, as having been a kind of paradoxical stasis of nuclear-family stability and cheesy normality.

Neither of these views is correct. What happened in the seventies was that, as at no other time before or since in our history, Americans—especially American women—were, for better and worse, free. Liberated, we cast aside the laws and limitations of the old familiar system to sail like *Voyager* out into the interstellar medium beyond. You can see it on the album covers of every band of meaty bohunks from Cleveland or Sheffield—the Raspberries, the Sweet, Aerosmith—who ever appeared with their hair piled high atop their heads and mascara on their eyes and their masculinity fully, if amusingly, intact. You can see it in a movie like the powerful documentary *51 Birch Street*, which is a kind of bitter and glorious paean to the way the seventies blew open the doors of one ordinary suburban American marriage, briefly offering to a conventionally trapped husband and wife new ways of being a man, a woman, a couple. You can see it in the sad contrast that Elizabeth Isadora Gold drew, in an essay for *The Believer*, between today's so-called chick lit and popular women's novels of the seventies like *Fear of Flying* and *The Women's Room*, in which women appeared, for the first time in all of modern literature, as genuine adventurers, sailing out into the blue as the heroes of their own sexual and intellectual quests, finding freedom and fulfillment and making fools of themselves.

The seventies were, finally, about *Voyager*, loopiness and all: about expanding consciousness by making contact, about translating yourself in all your particulars to a kind of universal message of love and desire and willingness to explore. They were about consciousness and self-consciousness (and sometimes loss of consciousness) and all the sense of genuine liberation, however goofy or naive or short-lived or untenable, that those things can impart. We can accept the invitation extended by those years to laugh at them, but in doing so, we are only getting in on the joke.

And God knows we have nothing in the line of liberation to make as counteroffer. Where women were once trapped inside a single narrative of child-rearing and housekeeping, the introduction of a second narrative of fulfillment through work and intellectual accomplishment has left them trapped in a kind of permanent ongoing guest role in both, able to star or to shine in neither. As for the supposed liberation of men, if all the socially viable ways of being a man (not counting those afforded and tolerated in gay culture) were languages or species of plants or animals, we would be living in a virtual monoculture. A dozen years from now, sometime around 2020 or so, when the atomic power plants carried on board the two *Voyagers* give out, all transmissions from the edge of things will cease, and the record that those two probes carry, of a moment's giddy will to expand the bright tiny circle of its consciousness, will drift on, in silence and darkness, waiting.

Subterranean

O ne June night in 1972, an early hurricane named Agnes rolled up the East Coast, raising rivers and drowning railroads and knocking out power all over the D.C. area. My family was living at my grandparents' house in Silver Spring that summer while we waited for construction to finish on a new house. My parents and grandfather were out for the evening, and my brother and I were left in the care of our grandmother, who seemed not to know what to do with us at seven o'clock on a Saturday night when the lights winked out and the television blacked over and she found herself alone with two bored boys only too eager to get busy in the darkness with the candles and the matches.

So she sent us to bed down in the basement, and though I remember being put out at the injustice of this decision, she was a grandmother in the quietly adamantine style, and there was no appeal and nothing to be done. My brother and I climbed into the convertible sofa bed we shared, and there was a clap of thunder, and I shut my eyes. A moment later I felt my father's hand on my shoulder, his voice soft and taut as if some unpleasant business was at hand.

"It's time to get up," he said. Somehow, as though in an instant, the entire night had passed—the only time in my life I remember having experienced such a passage—and it was morning. "But be careful."

My brother and I lowered our skinny legs over the sides of the sofa bed and plunged to our knees in cold rainwater. In the night, our basement room had been transformed, like Max's bedroom in *Where the Wild Things Are*, into a swimming pool, a rippled lake, a midnight sea. It was like magic, in all the delight and fearsomeness of the word. We might have been drowned or washed away. We might have paddled on sofa-cushion rafts to the far-off shores of our parents' bedroom. Magic, at both ends of the spectrum, is what happens in the basements of houses.

My grandfather had finished the basement sometime during the late 1950s in grooved plywood paneling and glossy black linoleum that, even on the hottest day of the summer, was as cold and hard as the frozen seas of Triton. With his tools, wiry arms, and pragmatic imagination, he had wrested four rooms and a bathroom out of a dank, dark hole under his house. There were two parlors furnished with cast-off and outmoded living room sets of the premodern era, the chairs creaky and stuffed with horsehair. In one parlor a neglected piano incrementally untuned itself, and in the other, on a small table designed expressly for the purpose, sat a great black piano of a telephone. It had a clacking iron dial that sprained your fingers, and when it rang like a firehouse alarm, you expected to find Alfalfa or Spanky on the other end of the line. The drawers of the end tables cataloged the entropy of board games, the history of typing supplies, the morphology of swizzle sticks and coasters. The basement bedroom in which my parents spent that hurricane summer had sheltered my mother's younger brother in the latter days of his adolescence and was decorated with a large black-and-white poster, popular during the late-sixties "nostalgia revival" (which no one then suspected would turn out to be permanent), of W. C. Fields playing a poker hand very close to the vest. Fields wore a sour expression, and there was always some residue of sourness in the bedroom, some discontent in the recollection of my uncle's time there, as if his tenure had carried an element of exile. Exile, too—the estrangement of the dungeon dweller, of the narrator of Richard Matheson's classic story "Born of Man and Woman"—is part of the enchantment of basements. At night my mother and father, only a few years away from separation and eventual divorce, would shut the door that did not quite shut and consider with growing discontentment the hand they had been dealt.

There were long-standing, sometimes bitter tensions in the other marriage under the roof that summer, and whenever my grandfather wanted to partake of the magic of exile, he would retreat to his underground workshop. It was dominated by a massive workbench built from pine and pegboard and fitted with a formidable screw vise. He had a table saw and a table drill, an extensive library of hand tools for working wood, metal, and leather, and a small laundry area, nominally my grandmother's territory but equipped with a sink and a stopcock to which you could attach the hose of a Bunsen burner. My grandfather, a patent lawyer, was an inventor in his own right, the holder of U.S. patent number 3826667 for something he called "magnetite paint." He was also an amateur photographer and maintained an improvised darkroom, with developing pans ranged alongside the steel laundry sink and a wooden photo enlarger of his own construction hunched like a big plywood mantis in a corner.

In those days the pages of comic books were frequently home to cutaway diagrams of secret lairs and headquarters, each with careful arrows pointing to the Sleeping Quarters, the Recreation Area, and—of course—the Research Laboratory. A couple of years after the night of the hurricane (and far sooner than my judgment or trustworthiness merited), my grandfather gave me the run of his Batcave. As soon as we arrived for a visit, I would go down there and begin to decoct, construct, rummage, demolish, assemble, snoop, waste time, get into trouble. I took apart broken machines and appliances and, in the name of my research, broke things that had nothing wrong with them. I spoiled splendid plans and managed to turn worthless junk into faithful scale models of things that no one had ever seen. I smashed my fingers with hammers, cut them with saws and chisels, burned them on the tips of soldering irons. I bled. I wept furtive tears over my injuries, which, like a wounded gangster, I was obliged to treat secretly lest I be banned from the basement forever. I went spelunking in deep closets and cabinets and picked out atonal versions of the theme from *Mission: Impossible* on the piano. Mostly, I lay around for hours on the musty sofa, utterly bored with myself and the universe, flooded as by a passing hurricane by the kind of tedium a child can feel only at his grandparents' house, wondering what it would be like to be somebody, somewhere, doing something, anything.

All of those activities, it seems to me now, helped form the basis for my life as a writer, a denizen of the basement of my soul. I suppose it is no accident that basements, hidden lairs, and underground settings have featured so routinely in my fiction: the gang rape of Happy the collie in the basement of the Bellwethers' house in *The Mysteries of Pittsburgh*, the macabre hideout of James Leer in *Wonder Boys*, the numerous hiding places and fortresses of solitude in *The Amazing Adventures of Kavalier & Clay*, the mysterious subterranean Untershtot of *The Yiddish Policemen's Union*, accessible by hole from the archetypical basement of the Hotel Zamenhof. In almost everything I've written, you can find buried treasuries, Batcaves and hidey-holes, half-forgotten underground worlds that perhaps encode the rapture and the bitterness of my own isolation.

The house that we eventually moved into after that summer at my grandparents' had a fine dank basement of its own, not so well finished but spectacularly equipped with a couple of earthen crawl spaces worthy of Montresor and Fortunato and a mysterious deep hole at its heart that was the burrow of a strange, rumbling creature known as the Sump Pump. As my parents' marriage fell apart, I took to spending more and more of my time down there, making stop-motion science-fiction epics with my Super 8 camera, curating and organizing and hiding inside the boxes of my comic book collection, listening to Casey Kasem count them down. It was a new basement, but it had the necessary residue of exile and mystery, and when you returned from a session down there, you could feel something following you, its hand at the back of your neck, racing you up to the light at the top of the stairs.

Now I live in Northern California, where, as if in obedience to some doctrine of spiritual health and equilibrium, houses do not, as a rule, have basements. My own children are reduced to the expedient—surely not to be disdained—of creating impromptu clubhouses from blankets, cushions, and chairs, or of seeking inspiration in the daylight quotidian fastness of their bedrooms. I wonder where it settles, the dark tide of magical boredom that was the source of all my own inspiration, in a house without a basement to catch and hold it like a cistern. I have often found myself wishing my kids had somewhere they could go to get away, get lost, feel frightened and safe at the same time. Someplace deep and buried, unsuspected by and inaccessible to any parent, and right underfoot.

Anyway, we built them a little tree house in the California buckeye in the backyard. It's bright, open, sky-bound, a crow's nest for the brigantine of their play. I worry that it is insufficiently dank, gloomy, remote, mysterious, but as they have filled it with random things, randomly broken and repaired, I have had reason to hope: hope that when they shut its bright green door, the world with all its puzzling business feels muffled and distant. Hope that they lie up there on their backs for hours, feeling tragic, and happy, and terribly, terribly bored.

swear I was twelve years old before my grandmother let me go into a men's room alone. If we were hanging around downtown Washington—and she was a great one for hanging around downtown, a flaneur in White Shoulders and a black sweater set— she used to smuggle me into the ladies' lounge at Garfinckel's department store when I had to go to the bathroom, even if getting there required a twenty-block walk, and when I say *smuggled*, I mean *pushed me like a dollyload of bricks while loudly exhorting me to cut in front of the blind woman with the oxygen tank.* It had to be Garfinckel's, no matter how long a schlep that meant, because only there, amid the caged parakeets and the splendor of the ladies' lounge, did the standard of hygiene come even remotely close to her own. The truth is that even Garfinckel's fell short. Before I was permitted to touch my flesh to the Garfinckel's toilet, she had to enter the stall like a fireman shouldering his way into a burning house, face grim and set, taking minimal sips of air through her nostrils, and wipe down the seat with a paper towel and the Lysol that at all times she kept in a small spray bottle in her handbag. When I was finished with my business, I was expected to summon her so that she could, with a single furious kick of her tiny foot, deploy the flush handle, flush handles being widely known to medical science as festering vectors of disease. Her spray bottle of Lysol came out on buses, too, to render the Naugahyde seats fit for contact, and she whipped it out whenever we went to sit on a bench in Dupont Circle for a session of her favorite pastime in that era: scowling at the "hippies" who gathered there and, in an undertone that was not especially low, mocking them. When she washed the dishes, she would encase each plate and fork in plastic wrap before returning it to the cabinet or drawer. She washed Dixie cups fresh from the package in soap and hot water. She had survived pogrom and transatlantic crossing and Depression and war, and she was not afraid of anything, least of all her son, my father, but she was terrified beyond reason of germs and bacteria.

When I was a kid I found this behavior fascinating, and as I got older, it was good for a laugh, but now I see that the poor woman was suffering from a form of obsessive-compulsive disorder: OCD, or XO9, as my younger son used to believe it was known. He was hearing a lot about XO9 and about my grandmother, because for a while my older son started believing that anything that happened to him on one side of his body—a pinch, a tickle, his mother's taking hold of his hand to cross a busy street—needed to happen right away on the other side of his body, too, or else he would feel "like I'm going to die." This particular form of the disorder, it turned out, meant he had symmetry issues, and there were other ones, including a brief but intense inability to get through five minutes of consciousness without mentioning cows at least once. These things mostly came and went, ramifying wildly, foliating like creepers through the kid's thoughts and, to some degree, the discourse of our family before fading with the help—help that my grandmother never received—of some fairly simple cognitive-therapy techniques and his grateful eagerness to try them. He was so relieved to learn that this thing could be named, could be talked about, that he began to feel better simply through the act of discussing it (which I think is why he consented immediately when I asked his permission to write about it).

This thing runs in families, and I can't help also seeing its signs in my father, an obsessively completist collector of stamps, coins, bubblegum cards, tobacco cards, autographs, Big Little Books, Ovaltine premiums, magazines, books, classical recordings—all kinds of stuff—the collections proliferating, branching off, some running their course, some enduring for decades. He's a man who cannot enter a room without aligning, or suppressing an overwhelming urge to align, the corners of books with the corners of tables they lie upon; a man whose neckties hang in a closet as neatly as the pipes of a church organ and whose desk drawers look like aerial photographs of a secret weapons facility in the Nevada desert.

My grandmother, my father, my son, and me. My few collections are incomplete, I have braved hellish shitholes without benefit or need of Lysol, and I have never experienced any bodily compulsions beyond those of my animal appetites. But I have this thing where I can't stop trying to fix something that's broken, some lock that won't open even with the right combination, some computer program that won't run or channel that won't TiVo—even if I have to stay up till four o'clock in the morning or miss out on the party in the next room to figure out what's wrong and how to repair it. Even if you resort to physically removing me from the vicinity of the problem, I will not be fully present in conversation or be able to sleep or find any savor in life whatsoever until I have solved it or, at long last, conceded defeat. Over the years certain random words or phrases, such as *Lampedusa*, *weasels*, and *Ted Kennedy*, have gotten trapped like flies in the casements of my brain and buzzed in fits for months or even years until some unknown hand threw up an invisible sash and they flew out. I must have said the word *monkeys* at least once a day for the past ten years, not counting references to actual simians or my children. And—this is not a boast—I rock. Davening, my wife calls it: steady, rapid, rhythmic rocking, sometimes fitful, sometimes continuous, from foot to foot when I'm standing, and from front to back when I'm sitting down. Rocking like a junkie who needs a fix, a madman on the subway, a devout Jew at prayer, a kid who really needs to pee.

I'm davening as I write these words, and it's always while I'm in the act of writing that the impulse to rock grows strongest, that the rocking feels the best, the most necessary and right. The more easily the words come, the more wildly I rock. When I consider the problem-solving nature of writing fiction—how whatever book I happen to be working on is always broken, stuck, incomplete, a

Yale lock that won't open, a subroutine that won't execute, yet day after day I return to it knowing that if I just keep at it, I will pop the thing loose—it begins to seem to me that writing may be in part a disorder: sheer, unfettered XO9. Look at Borges with his knives and his tigers, or Nabokov with his butterflies, or Irving with his bears, or Plath with her camps and her ovens; look at every writer, writing the same damn story, the same poem, returning endlessly to the same themes, the same motifs, the same locales, the same lost summer or girl or father, book after book. *Why do you keep writing about gay men who are friends with straight men?* people want to know. *Why are bad things always happening to dogs in your books? What's with all the sky similes? Why did you use the word* spavined, *like, seventeen times in one novel?* Sometimes I try to come up with sensible answers to these questions, logical explanations for these recurring tropes, motifs, and phrases, but in truth there's only one honest answer that a writer in the grip of XO9 can give:

I can't help it.

Sky and Telescope

W hen my father was a young pediatrician, he took care of a patient named Ira. My father had his favorite patients, and at the dinner table sometimes we used to hear about them. They tended to be either black or Jewish; Ira was the latter. He used to talk to my father about the stars.

"Ira was telling me today about Aldebaran," my father might say while he carefully smashed each carrot, pea, and cube of chuck roast in his dish of my mother's beef stew into a grayish paste. He is by nature a vegetarian but would never consider giving up meat. Hence he feels he needs to disguise it. "Apparently, it's a binary system."

This Ira kid was six, seven: my exact contemporary. Aldebaran, Betelgeuse, Tau Ceti. He knew whether they were blue or red. He understood the Doppler effect as it pertained to starlight. He even knew the Greek myths that underpinned so many of the constellations.

Now, I had strangely possessive feelings about mythology.

Once I came upon a copy of *D'Aulaire's Greek Myths* lying on a table in the school media center, lying there where any shmo could come along and pick it up and discover for himself the dark and vivid world that lay inside the covers of that book. Quickly, I returned it to the safe anonymity of the 398s.

Mythology was my territory. So I decided to horn in on Ira's.

I asked for a telescope. At Hannukah, one was duly provided, along with a small, dense, rather dry British volume entitled *Astronomy in Colour*. I have disappointed memories of that telescope. It was made of blue plastic and heavy gray cardboard, with a rickety metal tripod. It did not, as I had imagined, work by letting you put your eye up against the fiery flank of the universe itself. It had a small, bleary oculus that received a shimmery reflection from a tiny mirror that lived all alone at the bottom of the long cardboard tube. It had a focus knob that knowingly tormented you with seventeen different varieties of blur. It was not so much a telescope as a kind of antikaleidoscope, its interior vista endlessly static and dim. The book had a star chart and some interesting drawings of spacecraft and imaginary Saturnscapes. But its prose and its ideas were way over my head and of no real use, especially at night, in the dark, when I really needed the book. In the end, after some cursory study, I learned to find five or six of the most obvious constellations. Polaris, Betelgeuse. Venus and Mars.

My astronomical knowledge has not advanced very far since then. I get the Doppler effect. I know now what a binary system is. But I never showed the gift for astrophysics that I hoped to discover in myself, any more than I would later turn out to be a genius at chemistry, electric guitar, or the free-throw line. I never presented any threat to Ira. The starry heavens became a lifelong locus of insufficiency, but so is everything you love most, and that bitter memory has never stopped me from taking an interest in the night sky and its behavior.

Several years ago my wife bought me my second telescope. It is incredibly enormous. It is nuclear-powered, made of iron mined from an asteroid, and weighs seven metric tons. Its mirror is broad and brilliant and conveys an image of the moon so magnified that under a quarter of its visible surface more than fills the eyepiece. You can see the shadows of crater rims, the snaggled teeth of giant craters like Pythagoras and Herschel. The thing uses GPS and has a processor to allow it to know where it is and what you're looking at. When you train it on what appears to the naked eye to be a blank, black patch of sky, you find the oculus aglitter with stars and realize that beyond them could be seen, if you had a more powerful scope, more glittering specks of light and still more beyond them. And you feel a shallow shiver of how deep space really is.

Unfortunately, the thing requires a winch, a derrick, and a team of elephants to transport it. Also, I live in the city, in Berkeley, California, and when there's no fog to obscure it, our night sky is polluted with light. After my initial burst of enthusiasm for the telescope, I began to question its usefulness. By the time you, Tantor, and Queenie got the thing out to the front yard (where you could see about forty-two degrees of heavenly arc among the housetops and trees), you had dented a wall, stubbed your toe, pulled a muscle in your shoulder, and suffered a heart attack on the front porch. I fantasized about building a little observatory on top of the house where I could use the telescope without having to move it, but soon I realized that even if I could afford to do such a thing, there would be nothing much to see between the fog and the flooded sky once I got up there. So in time, the telescope was returned to its tuba-capable case and humped up to the attic to reproach me with my inadequacy like the heavens themselves.

This summer we shipped it to Maine. We've been coming here for the past few summers, and our good landlords let us store things in the basement of their house over the year, even enormous things like this telescope. The weather has been rotten, but tonight, as on four or five other fine nights, the sky just knocks you over. I used to share a house with a graduate student in astronomy who told me that when you first reach the top of Mauna Kea in Hawaii, where Cal maintains the Keck Observatory, your eyes are so starved for oxygen that they see almost nothing distinctive in the sky, a sparkly gauze. He described bending over to take a few deep breaths and then throwing his head back to take in with new oxygen-rich eyes, the newly blazing archipelago of lights. That is how the Maine sky can look sometimes to a city dweller. It dizzies you.

Jupiter has been working its nightly way across the sky all month. The word is debased, but when I first got Jupiter in the eyepiece, I thrilled at what I saw. Lined up to its left in a tidy row like ducklings swam four of its thirty-nine moons. The moons of Jupiter! Who would not thrill at the sight of them and the sound of their name? They were no bigger in the eyepiece than large stars to the naked eye, but they were there, unmistakably, and as I stood in the chill evening with crickets playing the summer offstage and mosquitoes grazing on my ankles, I felt as if I were there, too: out there, four hundred million miles away, orbiting that disappointed star.

That is a shared promise of telescopes and literature: to create an illusion of interstellar or interhuman travel within the confines of your own skull. Though I have always been aware of the connection between stories and constellations, between the beauty of the stars and the perhaps even greater beauty of their names, I never truly felt it until I looked through a first-rate instrument at an unspoiled sky.

"It kind of freaks me out to think about that, Dad," my older son said after I had him look through the telescope at one of those endlessly deep and star-packed regions of space that look empty to the naked eye. "I mean, we're so small."

"True," I said.

"We're, like, nothing."

"Well, yeah. Except to each other."

And then I pointed the telescope at Jupiter and its brood of moons and had him take a look, and he did a little thrilling himself. It's just so shocking somehow to see them there, plain as stars, when you can look at the same spot with no telescope and see a solitary speck of gold. "Think of Galileo," I told my son. "You and I know those moons are going to be there, but Galileo had no idea when he first saw them that they were going to be there. He just had the weird inspiration to point a newfangled set of lenses at the king of planets and check it out. Think how surprised he must have been!"

"Okay, that's awesome," my son agreed, backing away from the eyepiece. "What happens if we point it at the moon?"

Maybe he or one of my other children will turn out like Ira, to have the gift of stars. He or she will be able to look up at the sky and see not myths and legends and a history of failure but information, gases and voids, cold, infernal, luminous and pure. Or maybe my children will just look up and remember the weight of my hand on their shoulders as they stood beside me on a warm summer night, the rasp of my beard against their cheek, my voice soft at their ear, telling them, *Look*.

[VIII]

STUDIES IN PINK AND BLUE

Surefire Lines

My younger son asked me if I would teach him how to make a girl.

It was a fat curve, hung right out over the plate. But the boy was not yet five, and I knew that whatever I came back with would sail right over his head. So I decided to tell him the truth.

"I don't really know how to make a girl," I told him. "I've never been very good at it."

"You need to use more circles," suggested my older son. At the time he was a sophisticate of ten, but if my reply had been something like *Start by putting on a Barry White record*, it would have sailed over his head, too. "And make the circles, like, skinnier."

The boys in our house spend a lot of time drawing men. Not the girls—the girls mostly draw girls, but if their theme requires it, they will draw a necessary boy, and they never seem to run into any difficulties, or rather, the problems they encounter have nothing to do with their gender or that of the figures they're attempting to depict. The only trouble they have is the usual trouble with feet, noses, hands, poses, and proportions, the ones that dog anybody who tries to arrest and suggest the human form with a Flair pen or a No. 2 Ticonderoga. My older daughter is reasonably competent in drawing in the style of the Japanese comic books she loves, and apart from hairstyles and details of dress, there is not all that big a difference among the willowy and saucer-eyed youth who tend to populate those books, regardless of gender. My younger daughter is more into drawing hamsters, flowers, and disturbing hybrids thereof, so the question rarely arises. But for my sons and for me, it's pretty much an unvarying repertoire of male superheroes, male cyborgs, and male costumed action heroes of one kind or another.

"Is a girl superhero the same as a boy superhero?" the little one persisted, his tone betraying a certain forlornness. He was looking back and forth from me to the blank place on his piece of paper where he had been planning to put a drawing of Sue Storm, to round out his portrait of the Fantastic Four. Generally, he neglects or avoids the need to portray females in his artwork, but when it comes to the Fantastic Four, once you've done the rocks, the flames, and the rubbery arms, you basically have no choice in the matter. "Only she has some boobs?"

"Kind of," said the older brother, going a bit stony-eyed. His own inability to depict females, I imagined, was bitter knowledge that sometimes left him feeling forlorn, too. "Not exactly."

There was no doubt, I wanted to explain, that boobs were a big part—literally—of the female superhero package. Almost every superwoman apart from explicitly adolescent characters such as the original Supergirl or the X-Men's Kitty Pryde came equipped, as if by the nature of the job, with a superheroic rack. Furthermore, the usual way of a female superhero costume was to advertise the breasts of its wearer by means of décolletage, a cleavage cutout, a pair of metal Valkyrie cones, a bustier. In their unitards and tights, all comic book superheroes, male or female, are fundamentally tinted naked people, and this convenient fact has often tempted the (overwhelmingly male) anatomists of costumed heroes to let themselves get a tad carried away in carving the figureheads, as it were, of their dreamboats. Back in the early pre–Comics Code days, there had been a popular subgenre known as headlight comics, complete with its own genius, the mysterious African-American artist Matt Baker, whose lyrical mappings of Phantom Lady's planetary system continue to this day to haunt the fantasy life of some gray-haired old boys of the fifties. Today's female costumed characters tend to sport breasts so enormous that their ability simply to get up and walk, let alone kick telekinetic ass, would appear to be their most marvelous and improbable talent.

I remembered my childhood pencils-and-stapler comic book company with a couple of friends, one of whom, though not much of an artist, could do wonderful things with a bustier. His superladies never had faces (he couldn't do faces), and sometimes they had no hands or feet (feet are crazy hard), but they always had a Fantastic Two. And, as far as we were concerned at the time, that was almost enough. Almost.

"It's not just the boobs," I told my little son, sketching a quick

Sue Storm on my own sheet of drawing paper. "A lot of other things are different, too. The shoulders are narrower. The legs are, uh, longer. The, uh, the waist . . . the waist . . ."

We three looked at the snarl of lines I had made on the paper, at once tentative and overbold. We tried to see, with considerable charity on the boys' part, how the lines might resemble a stirring and heroical woman.

"What is a waist, anyway?" said the little one.

I started to feel forlorn myself. Over the years I have worked very hard to create in my fiction living, fiery female characters to match the life and fire of various real women I have known. I have endowed them as carefully and thoughtfully as I could with fragments of the histories and memories, with physical mannerisms, with traits of hair and complexion and even, occasionally, the recollected breasts of those living women. With each story, I have convinced myself as I told it that I was managing to portray a woman as strong and as fragile, as complicated and simple, as real, as the women who have been part of the story of my own life. It has not always been easy. I have struggled and written myself into corners and clichés, and resolutely shuffled paragraphs and memories. I have rewritten entire sections of a novel from a female character's point of view, just to see if I could do it, and in writing *The Amazing Adventures of Kavalier & Clay*, I spent months and months turning out some four hundred pages of close third-person narration about the sister of Sammy Clay, only to realize at some fatal point that (although quite flat-chested) she would never possess the marvelous, improbable power of getting up and walking around. This is a problem, I'm trying to say—I wanted to tell my boys—that I have been working on for a very long time. And yet each book that resulted has come under a certain amount of deserved criticism from female readers for being a boy's book, guy lit, for never quite presenting a female character to match the novel's men. A lot of this criticism tends to arise from the passionate female reader who is mother to the boys who were just then engaged in trying to learn something from my drawing of Sue Storm.

I looked at their faces, patiently waiting for me to come through for them. I had no idea why it should be so hard for me to depict women, whether with a pencil or a word processor. I find that I resent the difficulty on feminist grounds, for accepting it would seem to endorse the view that there is some mystic membrane separating male and female consciousness, some nebulous difference between men's and women's minds, when people are people and minds are minds and, if you want to get down to it, I don't really know or understand what goes on inside anybody's head apart from (in moments of grace) my own. I can't stand—I feel in all honesty that I was raised by a strong-willed, working mother in the heyday of feminism not to be able to stand—the retrograde pseudo-sensitive air of balderdash that seems to underlie the idea of a woman's heart being inaccessible to a man by virtue of their respective genders.

And yet there I sat, huddled down at the boys' end of the kitchen table with my sons, drawing big hypertrophied dudes in capes while, at the other end, the girls mutated their hamster flowers and posed their effete saucer-eyed teenage hermaphro-ninjas. I admired the girls' work vocally. But I knew that I didn't fully understand their reasons for wanting to draw what they were drawing and not what we boys all wanted to draw. The inescapable corollary of this knowledge has often seemed to be that while I also vocally admire my daughters themselves, I don't fully under-stand them, either. When one of them is feeling sad, or crushed, or furious, or anxious about a social situation in the classroom, I find myself unable to jolly or cajole or, worst of all, sympathize her out of it the way I can almost always manage to do with one of the boys. There is apparently an inherent callousness in me that fails to see the gravity or the angles in their gravest and most angular emotional situations or to understand the ins and outs of their complicated friendships. There is a mystery in those heads that I will never stop trying to solve, even if the very act of seeking solu-tion, of viewing women in terms of mystery, damns me forever to defeat and ineptitude.

So I turned to my son's drawing of the Fantastic Four to con-sider the blank spot on the far side of the Thing. And I gave up the art lesson for the day.

"I like your Invisible Woman," I told him, tapping the paper with the snake-oil panache of Hans Christian Andersen's tailor, hoping this line would not sail over his head. "Nice job."

"Oh!" said the little one, and for an instant, just before he grinned, he looked heartbreakingly confused. "I get it. Do you get it, Dad?"

I told him that I did. So sue me.

Cosmodemonic

Twenty-odd years and nine books after receiving my MFA in creative writing from the University of California, Irvine—and seventy years after the founding of the original MFA program, the Iowa Writers' Workshop—I still get questions about writing programs, as if my having come through one were a fluky detour like doing a hitch in a Goofy suit at Disneyland, and the institution itself a compound of rumor and scam. Journalists, critics, would-be students, regular people—they all have their doubts. Do writing workshops have any real value? Are they helpful to young writers? Do they perhaps unwittingly impose standards of style and subject matter on their graduates? And sometimes with a prosecutorial wink: Can anybody really be taught how to write? I have answers for these people. Put briefly: Yes; yes; I don't believe so but maybe; and yes. I wrote my first novel at Irvine, and one of my teachers there sent it to his agent, who found a publisher for the book. I'm kind of a poster boy for the more tangible benefits that a good writing program can bestow. And I have written elsewhere about the help and hard reading I received from my teachers and fellow students at UCI. But the most important thing that happened to me as a graduate student in creative writing had little directly to do with writing or publishing or agents or subject matter or style. When I started the program in 1985, I was a little shit; by the time I left Irvine, I was not just a published novelist, I was something that had begun, inwardly, to resemble a man.

This is not going to be an argument for some universal advantage conferred by the institution of the writing program; I am sure that graduate fiction workshops regularly turn out little shits by the dozens. I'm just going to try to figure out what might have happened to me while I was there.

Henry Miller, I think I should begin, was my great literary hero from the age of sixteen to about nineteen, and on the assumption that you haven't recently dipped into *Tropic of Cancer* or *Tropic of Capricorn* or *Black Spring* or the three volumes that make up *The Rosy Crucifixion*, I will summarize the work—and undersell it—according to my purpose here: It's basically one long novel about the exaltation and despair, in New York and Paris, of a little shit named Henry Miller. The Henry Miller presented in the fiction is a drunk, a cad, a loser, an angry, misogynistic fuckup with delusions of grandeur, oceanic ambition, lamentable habits of personal grooming, and the profound detestation of money and the material world that only the born cadger can maintain. " 'All I ask of life,' " as the narrator of *Tropic of Cancer* approvingly quotes his friend the novelist Van Norden, " 'is a bunch of books, a bunch of dreams, and a bunch of cunt.' " For a few crucial years that was my own secret little-shit motto—or so, at least, I told myself. I curated a personal pantheon of shit-heels—of musicians, actors, painters, writers, and directors from Charles Mingus to Pablo Picasso to Marlon Brando to Jean-Luc Godard—whose work or biography seemed replete with examples of the kind of giddily antisocial, why-the-fuck-not?, mock-Napoleonic self-involvement and hound-doggishness I thought I admired. The Miller hero—my hero—does what he wants, when he wants to, whether it makes any sense or not, even when doing so may hurt or bring sorrow to another. He is not merely contradictory like the rest of us but stubbornly, programmatically so. He is both a clown—a cuckold, capable of lacerating self-mockery—and a pompous bastard, self-important and "big-souled." He has the capacity for soaring transports of fellow feeling and the most petty acts of impotent revenge. Most of all, he treats the people around him—friends, enemies, lovers—with a cheerful, even lyric, contempt. They are the matter of his work, the furnishings of his dreams and nightmares, the objects of his fixations, the characters in the tawdry circus-cum-back-alley-opera of his life. If they are women, they are his cunts.

It's this last element, so crucial to the work of Henry Miller, that gives away the game. When I was twenty years old, the following statement would have at once outraged me and made sense to me: *You know nothing about women.* It's just a sappy and worthless generalization to me now, empty of meaning. But at the time I thought *women* was a category, a field, like post-Parker jazz or the varieties of marijuana, that you could study and master and "know something about." If you are a callow young man at twenty—and

I think the man of twenty pretty much defines the term—then your callowness consists almost entirely in this type of belief, that life is made up of mastering the particulars, memorizing the lineups, accumulating the trivia and lore, in knowing how to trace the career of drummer Aynsley Dunbar or get a girl to go to bed with you and your best friend, as an expression of your existential freedom and complete disregard for the fact that she is a person, and she likes you or him, and you're actually kind of breaking her heart.

Misogyny comes naturally to a young man in his late teens; it is a function of the powerful homosocial impulses that flower along Fraternity Row, that drove the mod movements of the mid-sixties and the late seventies, that lie at the heart of every rock band formed by men of that age. Because I was bright and a would-be artiste, my own misogyny wore a beret, as it were, and quoted Nietzsche. But it was just—and I don't mean to excuse it with that adverb—garden-variety late-teenage, homosocial misogyny as practiced by young men all over the world. It certainly didn't constitute any kind of philosophical program or postmodern structure of morality. It was a phase, a plankton bloom in the brain, a developmental stage, albeit one that found ample reinforcement, if not glorification, in culture both popular and highbrow, in the Rolling Stones's "Stupid Girl" and Woody Allen's best movies, in Jorge Luis Borges, in William Shakespeare.

I don't know how much of this Millerite misogyny was reflected in my writing at the time—a fair amount, I suppose. You can see clear traces of it in The Mysteries of Pittsburgh. And I don't know if

I would have emerged from this stage on my own in time. People have argued more or less persuasively that our culture (okay, our entire civilization) is founded on misogyny, or that in its current state it represents a collective case of arrested adolescent development, and I guess even a man who outgrows the little shit never leaves him entirely behind. But when I showed up at Irvine to start my first year as the youngest member of the MFA fiction workshop, I was not ready for what I found there: a roomful of grown-ups, over half of them women. Some of these women were married; one of them had a grown child. Without taking themselves half as seriously as I did, they were all twice as serious about what they were doing. They were better read, more disciplined, more widely traveled, and far less impressed with me than I was. If they were feminists—and I am sure that each of them was—they were practiced and experienced feminists, versed in theory and tested if not hardened by the real world. And most of these women, even those who were not much older than I was, were finished—long since finished—with the charms, real or imagined, of little shits.

I want to stress that what followed was not just some rude awakening or shakedown cruise where I tried to get these women to sleep with me and one by one they shot me down. Okay, so there was some of that, but the fact of the matter is that I had been on a losing streak with women for a long time—at least it felt like a long time—and had already begun to see reflected, in the eyes of some of the girls I had gotten nowhere with, a certain weariness with, or distrust of, or even distaste for, my displays of Miller-esque big-souled callowness. What happened at Irvine was that I found myself for three hours once a week in a room where my traditional enterprise—the great Van Norden dream—was entirely and thrillingly beside the point. We had work to do, and we were lucky enough to have been granted a couple of years of freedom and time to do it. The people in the workshop, but especially the women, and especially the women who were in the full middle of their lives, knew—they could testify to—how rare and marvelous such a gift was. They had left real jobs, made real sacrifices, to come to Irvine. They had mortgages and health problems, troubled marriages, debts, and obligations. And so I was obliged, or at least I felt I was, to rise to the standard they set: in their writing, for the treatment of human emotion and relationships; in their lives, for seizing this chance to learn and share and get immersed in the work; and in the workshop itself, women and men, for undertaking that collective work with respect, with charity, with tolerance, and above all—most frightening to me at the time—with no patience for the pretense and callowness and trite antisocial pose of some little shit. In the end, I think that's the only cure for the little shit: regular exposure to the healing rays of healthy disillusion, in particular the hard-earned skepticism of grown women. Call it the Yoko Ono effect.

We are accustomed to repeating the cliché, and to believing, that "our most precious resource is our children." But we have plenty of children to go around, God knows, and as with Doritos, we can always make more. The true scarcity we face is of practicing adults, of people who know how marginal, how fragile, how finite their lives and their stories and their ambitions really are but who find value in this knowledge, even a sense of strange comfort, because they know their condition is universal, is shared. You bring your little story to the workshop, and sometimes it works and sometimes it doesn't; and then you're gone, and it's time for somebody else to have the floor.

Boyland

We were lying on the beach, reading our novels, surrounded by other parents reading their novels, all of us vaguely aware of our children's whereabouts and happy with that vagueness. The paramount amenity at this resort on the Kona Coast of Hawaii's Big Island, with its two modest swimming pools, its picturesquely turbid lagoon, its unremarkable dive shack stocked with snorkel gear and surf and boogie boards, its half-dozen sea kayaks, its quaint old badminton lawn and shuffleboard court—no TV, no phones, no arcade, no Eurofascist Club Med mass eurythmics, no swim-up bar, no waterslides, tightrope, parasailing, or Jet Skis—was a careful allowance for parental carelessness. Our little ones were nearby, audible, in sight if you looked up from your book but not underfoot, digging in the sand or eating it, flirting on sandpiper legs with the edges of the surf.

But the big ones—we had no idea. They were off together somewhere. Gangs of boys, gangs of girls, mixed groups and shifting constellations of duos and triads, solitary wanderers haunting the fringes, our children spent their days largely out of our sight, monitored deftly but loosely by the parental collective, reporting only for meals or to put on a rash guard, dwelling for one magic week in a near-simulacrum of the kind of world, populated, legislated, enchanted, and tormented by kids, in which we ourselves had spent our entire childhoods. The price in dollars for this brief taste of the freedom we otherwise routinely denied the children broke my heart almost as much as the alacrity with which they took to it. At some point my oldest daughter showed up to get more sunscreen or dump her goggles, and to tell us that some boys out at the farthest extreme of the lagoon had been amusing themselves by catching fish and then ripping them apart at the gills.

My wife was properly horrified and disgusted by this report, as I was; she was also shocked and outraged, reactions I did not share.

"What's not to believe?" I said. "Boys. Animals. Cruelty." I remarked that in the filing cabinet of my childhood, that was the label on one very long drawer.

"You go tell those boys, the next time you see them doing anything like that, honey," my wife told our daughter, "you tell them hurting animals is how psychopaths get their start. Serial killers."

"Yes," I said. "Particularly if you're trying to inspire more violence to fish."

"They would love that," agreed our older son, who had materialized from some corner of the resort, salt-streaked, muddy, shock-headed, and semi-lapsed himself into a state of happy nine-year-old barbarity. "They think serial killers are awesome."

"You would never do anything like that, would you?" my wife asked him. "You would never hurt animals."

Our son shook his head, looking offended by the question. He might have been lying, but my knowledge of his belief system, composed of equal parts off-kilter *Far Side* animal-centrism and a dark Captain Nemoesque contempt for humanity, inclined me to think he was telling the truth. Gigantic fish pulling the limbs from cruel little boys, that might be something you could get him to sign on for.

"Did you ever do stuff like that?" my wife asked me. "Hurt things and kill things when you were a boy?"

I had been anticipating this question, or rather, I had already begun to put it to myself, with an initial certainty that the answer must be no, since no such incident, with its attendant vibration of shame or remorse, came to mind. But now I gave it some proper thought, because I felt that those boys—nice enough kids, it had seemed to me, not sullen or loutish—had called into question not only the great lost freedom of childhood that I have spent so much time lamenting and evoking but, in my own absence of outrage or surprise at the incident, the morality, indeed the sanity, of my gender itself.

I riffled through the deck of my memories of idle afternoons long ago, hours spent in the woods behind our house, in the far reaches of a schoolyard deserted on a Sunday, along the streams and in the basements of Columbia, Maryland. As I shuffled memories, I stopped a moment at every spot of darkness and searched it for the presence of violence to animals. I came up with neighborhood dogs that I had feared or been bitten by—even today I could draw you a map of how to avoid them. A hamster my brother and I had surprised in the act of devouring its young. Something horrible that I came upon one day behind a veterinarian's office, blind and bloody and unborn. Suicidal zebrafish that had leaped to their deaths behind the credenza in our living room on which their aquarium sat; it was nothing but popeye and ick and bedraggled floaters that came to mind when I thought about that tank. Birds that smashed against our back windows. Our miniature schnauzer gamely dragging himself across the floor, hind legs crushed by the car that had run him over. A dead bat cobwebbed like a dried leaf in a gauzy window curtain. The little red gifts left scattered around by neighborhood cats: half-eaten mice, gnawed moles, the heads of sparrows. It occurred to me that for all my liberty to wander as a child, without animals I would have known nothing of carnage or violent death. This seemed somehow like a strangely mixed blessing.

"I guess I killed innocent bugs," I said. I was thinking of the cicada summer of 1970, when just walking down the street, you couldn't help crushing dozens of the stupid things under the soles of your PF Flyers. We fed them to the local dog that would eat them. We braked our bicycles on patches of them, smearing grisly stripes across the sidewalk. We hit them with baseball bats and golf clubs. We burned them with the lenses of magnifying glasses. Now that I thought about it, I had set fire to plenty of grasshoppers that way, too, watching their outraged legs wriggle as a smoking hole dazzled like a gem embedded in their abdomens. "Maybe a lot of bugs. And I knew boys who would do worse."

There were the boys who used to get together sometimes to fit out fish and frogs with firecrackers and lob those living grenades; there were the boys who went after sparrows and robins with BB guns, wounding far more than they mercifully killed. And laughing as the flustered bird lurched away.

"So you're saying that kind of thing is normal," my wife said. "Your attitude is just 'Boys will be boys.'"

"I'm not saying it's normal or acceptable. Yes, I do think boys will be boys. I guess I'd just never try to argue that's a good thing."

Boys will be boys, and men will be men, and killing fields are killing fields, and Rwanda is Rwanda, and Mountain Meadows is Mountain Meadows, and you gang us up and look the other way and some kind of bad activity might very well occur to us. Or it might not. One thing I never learned in all my years of meandering unsupervised through the world of boys was how to predict what they might do, singly or in groups, what startling kindness or humdrum cruelty they might choose to engage in. But I supposed it never hurt to have somebody around—maybe a bigmouthed bossy girl—to tell them they were a bunch of psycho losers.

I looked at my son, who was getting even less of an opportunity to contemplate this mystery than I had gotten, and then at my wife, who was waiting for me to answer for our crimes. I nodded and turned to my daughter.

"Next time," I told her, "you just go ahead and get in there and tell those boys whatever you want."

A Textbook Father

Some boys were playing in the hallway: eleven, twelve years old, pushing one another around in a wheeled desk chair. Shirttails untucked, yelling, taunting, acting like idiots. Taking turns being the fortunate fool in the chair who goes careening down the linoleum and crashes into the wall and falls out and gets hurt and fakes like he's okay. They were loud, unruly, locked in to the clatter of the wheels, the delighted scream of the idiot at the moment of impact, the collective enterprise of wasting time with a hint of violence. They were, I believe, happy.

Then my daughter entered the scene, passing from one doorway to another across and down the hall. She was twelve then, going on thirteen, tall, leggy, not exactly graceful—no dancer—but with a distinct air of confidence in her gait, of knowing where she was going and how to get there. I'm not sure she even noticed the boys and their chair, perhaps because the instant she entered the hallway, they all fell completely silent and stood there gaping at her, motionless, sagging like the fingers of an empty glove.

They weren't having fun anymore. She had kicked their power cord right out of the wall just by walking past.

Nobody ogled or leered at her. There was no Tex Avery business with extruded eyeballs or the unspooled flapping window shades of their tongues. Nothing unseemly or overtly sexual at all, just a bunch of boys standing around blinking as this girl sauntered by. And yet the moment, which I happened to catch sight of through a doorway, made me really uncomfortable. For a while everything about my daughter's entrance into puberty, her emerging new self and the concomitant interest of boys in her, discomfited me. And the part of it that made me squirm the most was how depressingly trite my discomfort was.

I am not a prude. I like sex; I respect sex; I have enjoyed sex, not without interruptions, losing streaks, and dry spells, for almost thirty years. I don't care to give sex any more credit than it deserves, nor do I necessarily prefer it at any given moment of the day to drugs, rock and roll, watching *The Wire*, or the sight of a paper packet filled with well-salted pommes frites still hissing with oil from the fryer. I like the dirtiness of sex, the smell of it, the measured violence and tenderness. I like thinking about sex. I don't begrudge sex or its indisputable pleasures to anyone in any variation that consenting partners can safely attempt or devise—not even to my children, when the time comes and they are of age, well informed, and emotionally ready. My wife and I vaccinated our daughter early against the human papilloma virus, a gesture that encompassed or presaged or at least sought to face up to the nature and the dangers of her eventual life as a sexual being. I believe that sexual freedom is good for all women, including my daughters, and good therefore also for the men who may one day be their partners; that sexual hypocrisy and repression are inherently evil; and that the protective ministrations and censoriousness of fathers are at best harmful to daughters and at worst the mark of the same kind of deep human ickiness that brought us the story of Lot and his daughters. And yet there I was, scowling at those boys in the hallway, feeling an obscure and altogether clichéd urge to go after them with a large mallet, because I didn't like them looking at my daughter that way—or any way at all.

Was that the kind of father I had turned out to be? Standing on the front porch with my shotgun under one arm, cartoonishly interrogating my daughters' cartoonish dates as they sat with a boxed cartoon corsage covering their cartoon boners? Fumbling with a show of jocular pedantry or saggy would-be hipness through every "little chat" with her about menarche or masturbation?

How embarrassing! and above all, in my lamentable sense of embarrassment over the whole business! when the first box of junior-size tampons made its appearance in the house—a bit prematurely, as it turned out—and in spite of my having been raised by a frank 1970s-style mother who saw to it that I understood clearly the laws and equipment of menstruation, and my having lived intimately with women and their periods since I was not quite eighteen years old, I suffered the tritest fatherly panic imaginable.

"Do these fucking things come with instruction books?" I cried to my wife. "Oh my God, what if you die the day before she gets her period?"

"Relax," my wife said, putting her arm around my shoulder and adopting a textbook condescending-yet-patient wife cartoon tone. "It's very simple."

I have no idea what she said after that, because I was too busy pretending to pretend that I understood. I am sure it is very simple indeed, though there is still and I suppose there will always be a fundamental mystery inherent in the word *applicator* that I will never fully grasp. But brassieres—I'm sorry. Cup size, wires, padding, straps, clasps, the little flowers between the cups: You need a degree, a spec sheet. You need breasts. I don't know what you need to truly understand brassieres, and what's more, I don't want to know. I'm sorry. Go ask your mother.

There you have it: the most flagrant cliché imaginable. As I utter it, I might as well reach for a trout lure, a socket wrench, the switch on my model train transformer. This may be the fundamental truth of parenthood: No matter how enlightened or well prepared you are by theory, principle, and the imperative not to repeat the mistakes of your own parents, you are no better a father or mother than the set of your own limitations permits you to be. And that set is your heritage, the pinched and helpless legacy of all the limited mothers and fathers whose fumblings, evasions, and shortcomings led, by some dubious accidental magic, to the production of you. It turns out there are only nine different ways of being a father, and eight of them are distinguishable from one another only by trained experts from Switzerland, and the ninth is exactly like the others, only more so. Sooner or later, you will discover which kind of father you are, and at that moment you will, with perfect horror, recognize the type. You are the kind of father who fakes it, who yells, who measures his children with greatest accuracy only against one another, who evades the uncomfortable and glosses over the painful and pads the historic records of his sorrows and accomplishments alike. You are the kind who teases and deceives and toys with his children and subjects them to displays of rich and manifold sarcasm when—as is always the case—sarcasm is the last thing they need. You are the kind of father who pretends knowledge he doesn't possess, and imposes information with implacable gratuitousness, and teaches lessons at the moment when none can be absorbed, and is right, and has always been right, and always will be right until the end of time, and never more than immediately after he has been wrong. And when your daughter's body begins to betray her, and her sky flickers in the distance with the heat lightning of sex, you clear your throat and stroke your chin whiskers and tell her to go ask her mother. You can't help it—you're a walking cliché.

TACTICS OF WONDER AND LOSS

The Omega Glory

I was reading, in an issue of *Discover*, about the Clock of the Long Now. Have you heard of this thing? It is going to be a system of gigantic mechanical computers, slow, simple, and ingenious, marking the hour, the day, the year, the century, the millennium, and the precession of the equinoxes with a huge orrery to keep track of the immense ticking of the six inner planets on their great orbital mainspring. The Clock of the Long Now will stand at least sixty feet tall and cost tens of millions of dollars, and when it's completed, its designers and supporters—among them visionary engineer Danny Hillis, a pioneer in the concept of massively parallel processing, Whole Earth mahatma Stewart Brand, and British composer Brian Eno (one of my household gods)—plan to hide it in a cave in Great Basin National Park in Nevada, a day's hard walking from anywhere. Oh, and it's going to run for ten thousand years. That is about as long a span as separates us from the first makers of pottery, among the oldest technologies we have. Ten thousand years is twice as old as the pyramid of Cheops, nearly twice as old as that mummified body found preserved in the Tyrolean Alps, one of the oldest mummies ever uncovered. The Clock of the Long Now is being designed to thrive under regular human maintenance during the whole of that span, though during periods when no one is around to tune it, the giant clock will contrive to adjust itself. But even if the Clock of the Long Now fails to last that long, even if it breaks down after half or a quarter or a tenth of that span, this mad contraption will already have long since fulfilled its purpose. Indeed, the Clock may accomplish its greatest task before it is ever finished, perhaps without ever being built at all. The point of the Clock of the Long Now is not to measure out the passage into their unknown future of the race of creatures that built it. The point of the Clock is to revive and restore the whole idea of the Future, to get us thinking about the Future again, to the same degree we used to, if not in quite the same way, and to reintroduce the idea that we don't just bequeath the future—though we do, whether we think about it or not. We also, in the very broadest sense of the first-person-plural pronoun, inherit it.

Strictly speaking, the Sex Pistols were right: There is no future, for you or for me. By definition, the future does not exist. "The Future," whether you capitalize it or not, is always only an idea, a proposal, a scenario, a sketch for a mad contraption that may or may not work. The Future is a story we tell, a narrative of hope, dread, or wonder. And it's a story that we've been pretty much living without for a while now.

Ten thousand years from today: Can you imagine that day? Okay, but *do* you? Do you believe the Future is going to happen?

If the Clock works the way it's supposed to—if it lasts—do you believe there will be a human being around to witness, let alone mourn, its passing; to appreciate its accomplishment, its faithfulness, its immense antiquity? What about five thousand years from now or even five hundred? Can you extend the horizon of your expectations for our world, for our complex of civilizations and cultures, beyond the lifetime of your own children, of the next two or three generations?

I was surprised when I read about the Clock of the Long Now at how long it had been since I had given any thought to the state of the world ten thousand years hence. At one time I was a frequent visitor to that imaginary mental locale. And I don't mean merely that I regularly encountered the Future in the pages of science-fiction novels or comic books, or when watching a TV show like *The Jetsons* (1962) or a movie like *Beneath the Planet of the Apes* (1970). The story of the Future was told to me when I was growing up, not only by popular art and media but by public and domestic architecture, industrial design, school textbooks, theme parks, and public institutions from museums to government agencies. I heard the story of the Future when I looked at the space-ranger profile of the Studebaker Avanti, at the burnerless range top of a Jenn-Air stove, at Tomorrowland through the portholes of the Disneyland monorail, at the tumbling plastic counters of my father's Seth Thomas Speed Read clock. I can remember writing a report in sixth grade on hydroponics; if you had tried to tell me then that by 2005 we would still be growing our vegetables in dirt, you would have broken my heart.

Even thirty years after its purest expression on the covers of pulp magazines like *Amazing Stories* and, supremely, at the New York World's Fair of 1939, the collective cultural narrative of the Future remained largely an optimistic one of the impending blessings of technology and the benevolent computer-assisted meritocracy of Donald Fagen's "fellows with compassion and vision." But by the early seventies, it was not all farms under the sea and family vacations on Titan. Sometimes the Future could be a total downer. If nuclear holocaust didn't wipe everything out, then humanity would be enslaved to computers, by the ineluctable syllogisms of "the Machine." My childhood dished up a series of grim cinematic prognostications best exemplified by the Hestonian trilogy that began with the first *Planet of the Apes* (1968) and continued through *The Omega Man* (1971) and *Soylent Green* (1973). Images of future dystopia were rife in rock albums of the day, as on David Bowie's *Diamond Dogs* (1974) and Rush's 2112 (1976), and the futures presented by seventies writers of science fiction such as John Brunner tended to be unremittingly or wryly bleak.

In the aggregate, stories of the Future presented an enchanting ambiguity. The other side of the marvelous Jetsons future might be a story of worldwide corporate-authoritarian techno-tyranny, but the other side of a postapocalyptic mutational nightmare landscape like that depicted in *The Omega Man* was a landscape of semi-barbaric splendor and unfettered (if dangerous) freedom to roam, such as I found in the pages of Jack Kirby's classic adventure comic book *Kamandi: The Last Boy on Earth!* (1972–76). That ambiguity and its enchantment, the shifting tension between the bright promise and the menace of the Future, was in itself a kind of story about the ways, however freakish or tragic, in which humanity (and, by implication, American culture and its values, however freakish and tragic) would continue in spite of it all. *Ee'd plebnista*, intoned the devolved Yankees in the *Star Trek* episode "The Omega Glory" (1968); they had somehow managed to hold on to and venerate as sacred gobbledygook the preamble to the Constitution, *norkohn forkohn perfectunun*. All they needed was a Captain Kirk to come and add a little interpretive water to the freeze-dried document, and the American way of life would flourish again.

I don't know what happened to the Future. It's as if we have lost our ability or our will to envision anything beyond the next hundred years or so, as if we lack the fundamental faith that there will be any future at all beyond that not too distant date. Or maybe we stopped talking about the Future around the time that, with its microchips and its twenty-four-hour news cycles, it arrived. Some days when you pick up the newspaper, it seems to have been co-written by J. G. Ballard, Isaac Asimov, and Philip K. Dick. Human sexual reproduction without male genetic material, digital viruses, identity theft, robot firefighters and minesweepers, weather control, pharmaceutical mood engineering, rapid species extinction, U.S. presidents controlled by boxes mounted between their shoulder blades, air-conditioned empires in the Arabian desert, transnational corporatocracy, reality television: Some days it feels as if the imagined future of the mid–twentieth century were a kind of checklist, one from which we have been too busy ticking off items to bother extending it. Meanwhile, the dwindling number of items remaining on that list—interplanetary coloni- zation, sentient computers, quasi-immortality of consciousness through brain download or transplant, a global government (fas- cist or enlightened)—have been represented and re-represented so many hundreds of times in films, in novels, and on television that they have come to seem, paradoxically, already attained, already known, lived with, and left behind. Past, in other words.

This is the paradox that lies at the heart of our loss of belief or interest in the Future, which has in turn produced a collective cultural failure to imagine that Future, any future, beyond the rim of a couple of centuries or the void of planetary catastrophe. The Future was represented so often and for so long in the terms and characteristic styles of so many historical periods from, say, Jules Verne forward that at some point the idea of the Future—along with the cultural appetite for it—came itself to feel like some- thing historical, outmoded, no longer viable or attainable. One possible turning point here was *Star Wars* (1977), with its setting in the remote past, its western gunfights and World War I dogfights, its deliberate evocation of the styles and conventions of *Metropolis* (1927) and old Flash Gordon serials. After *Star Wars*, every cine- matic Future has drawn heavily on the Futures imagined by previ- ous historical eras. Even what is perhaps our era's most heavily subscribed, culturally predominant narrative of the Future—the crypto-Christian vision of the End presented in the "Left Behind" series—is derived from imagery and narrative, some of which is by now almost two thousand years old.

If you ask my older son about the Future, he essentially thinks the world is going to end, and that's it. Most likely global warming, he says—floods, storms, desertification—but the possibility of viral pandemic, meteor impact, or some kind of nuclear exchange is not alien to his view of the days to come. Maybe not tomorrow or a year from now. The kid is more than capable of generating a full head of optimistic steam about next week, next vacation, his next birthday. It's only the world a hundred years on that leaves his hopes a blank. My son seems to take the end of everything, of all human endeavor and creation, for granted. He sees himself as living on the last page, if not in the last paragraph, of a long, strange, and bewildering book. If you had told me when I was his age that a kid of the future would feel that way—and what's more, that he would see a certain justice in our eventual extinction, would think the world was better off without human beings—it would have been even worse than hearing that his world would offer no hydroponic megafarms, no human colonies on Mars, no personal jet packs for everyone. That truly would have broken my heart.

When I told my son about the Clock of the Long Now he listened very carefully, and we looked at the pictures on the Long Now Foundation's Web site. "Will there really be people then, Dad?" he said. "Yes," I told him without hesitation, "there will." I don't know if that's true, any more than do Danny Hillis and his colleagues, with the beating clocks of their hopefulness and the orreries of their imaginations. But in having children—in engendering them, in loving them, in teaching them to love and care about the world—parents are betting, whether they know it or not, on the Clock of the Long Now. They are betting on their children, and their children after them, and theirs beyond them, all the way down the line from now to the 130th century. If you don't believe in the Future, unreservedly and dreamingly, if you aren't willing to bet that somebody will be there to cry when the Clock finally, ten thousand years from now, runs down, then I don't see how you can have children. If you have children, I don't see how you can fail to do everything in your power to ensure that you win your bet and that they and their grandchildren and their grandchildren's grandchildren will inherit a world whose perfection can never be accomplished by creatures whose imagination for perfecting it is limitless and free. And I don't see how anybody can force me to pay up on my bet if, in the end, I turn out to be wrong.

Getting Out

I met David Foster Wallace only once, at UCLA in October 2004, when we appeared together with a number of other writers at a fund-raiser for the Kerry campaign. I doubt we exchanged more than twenty-nine words, none of them memorable, at least by me. He struck me as shy and uncomfortable in the setting: in the big backstage area at Royce Hall, a whole bunch of people milling around, Cheney debating Edwards on a television in a corner and Wallace left to himself, getting ready to go out and, at least by virtue of his presence in front of a largish audience, endorse the doomed ticket. In my memory, he is wearing the trademark always unlikely bandanna, but this image may be the influence of too many author photos. The political nature of the event and Wallace's participation in it seemed to trouble him, I thought. Not that he wanted anything other than to see Bush defeated. He just seemed suspicious of the whole enterprise—a twenty-first century presidential election—and of his own role as a putative agent therein. The kindness and politeness he showed to me and my wife was exemplary, but I admit I was intimidated by him. If you had read his formidable work, especially *Infinite Jest* (which I had failed twice to finish), then it was hard, at least for me, not to feel that Wallace easily could have made more out of you, found more to say on your behalf and by way of explanation of you, than you had so far managed to do for yourself. I felt that he was disappointed in me, or maybe in the fact that I evidently cared so much what he thought about me. I felt in the two minutes that fate allotted me to pass in the company of David Foster Wallace, I had somehow let him down. Indeed, when he followed me on that evening's program, coming onstage to read to us (a story, as I recall, or anyway, a piece of a story, about a weird boy's awful birthday party), the first thing he said into the microphone was something like "Oh, great, another white man with glasses." Maybe he was disappointed in us both.

So I did not know David Foster Wallace. I thought of him as a peer, but one removed from me by a number of coextensive distances, of space, of aesthetic, of temperament. I had found intense pleasure in his essays and would have been prepared to defend his work as crucial if not signal to our time. But his death has been the focus of my thoughts for the past few days, as if, in a happier world, I had been given the opportunity to know him as a friend. I keep coming back to him in that last moment, hour, day, year of his life, trying to understand and to see and, in some awful way, to imagine the finite series of thoughts that led him to take his own life.

My first impulse is to assert that suicide is an idea alien to my way of thinking. I guess that's mostly a matter of wiring and fortune. So far, knock wood, I have not suffered enough from any hurt, or sunk deeply enough into any hole, to wish that my life, my precious life, were over. At my worst moments, in the darkest, rawest hours nearest to perdition, I have always found myself comforted by a cool voice inside me whispering that nothing, not even unbearable sorrow, lasts forever. I have that idiot optimism that is one quarter ruthless and one half mindless: a dangerous and, in its own way, often fatal trait. And yet the image of suicide fills my work from the first novel to the last. Self-interment, self-negation, and the hope, illusory or certain, of escape from the pain of life make up a central thematic thread in *The Amazing Adventures of Kavalier & Clay*. The plot of *The Yiddish Policemen's Union* turns entirely on the mystery of self-murder. One of the heroes of *Gentlemen of the Road* is almost habitually prevented from killing himself only by his hemp pipe and the careful management of his best friend, and in *Wonder Boys*, Grady Tripp has never outrun the shadow of the suicidal horror writer August Van Zorn. I keep coming back to the subject, to a degree that strikes me now, given my supposed alienation from the act of suicide, as hard to explain.

My wife suffers from bipolar disorder, which from time to time has given her ready access to the pain and hopelessness required to cast a comparative luster on the prospect of oblivion. When she gets low, I always imagine her mind as a child folding itself inside one of those three-panel department-store mirrors, past and future reaching off in an endless, dim, identical prospect of days, with her own head always right smack there in the way. In early 2005 she posted an entry to her then-blog in which she very calmly and methodically laid out the nature of bipolar II, its burdens and unexpected benefits. In this post she cited twice a statistic alleging that one in four people diagnosed with bipolar II eventually kills him- or herself.

I was in Little Rock, Arkansas, at the time, in a low mood myself (no disrespect to Little Rock) because it was gray and chilly, and George W. Bush was still and apparently forever president of the United States, and I was alone in Little Rock (sorry, Little Rock), and far from home. I had been over to visit the then-new Clinton presidential library, where they had two electoral maps showing the vast swaths of blue that went for Bill Clinton in 1992 and 1996, a sight that filled me with wonder and despair. Then I went back to my grim hotel room in the rain. The world was all gray sky and pressboard veneer and the map of Everything was always going to be red, red, red. I tried to call home, but no one was there. So, as if to reach her, I went online and checked my wife's blog.

I was shocked by what I found there, and upset. I called her cell phone and reached her, but she was in the middle of seven different things, driving the car while wiping someone's nose while running to an appointment while talking to me. She sounded fine; she was being brave, handling the job, doing fine without me. I hung up feeling that I must have been overreacting to the post. I persuaded myself that in my own funk, I had been reading in, imagining, the hints of suicide in her post, or that if such hints were there, she could not really mean them to be taken seriously. She had a well-known tendency to exaggerate states of outrage and emotion. Surely she was only fooling around, I told myself, albeit in a dark vein. That is the way you tend to think when, like me, your optimism is of the idiot variety. It did not occur to me that suicide was itself a kind of final and unanswerable exaggeration. Surely we have no way of knowing that things cannot possibly get any worse, any more than we can know for certain that the situation will not—perhaps very soon—improve. To declare one or the other by taking one's own life is a patent exaggeration unsupported by any evidence: a lie. And yet it remains, by its nature, irrefutable.

When I returned the next day from my trip, I learned to my horror that my wife had come very near to swallowing a bottle of pills the night before. Only a middle-of-the-night phone call from a friend in Israel who had read the blog post and who insisted—staying on the line to see that she did it—that my wife call her psychiatrist and wake him up interrupted the involute downward flow of Ayelet's mood to the bottom. This friend was one of several people, including a number of strangers on the Internet, who called or e-mailed her with some sense of urgency to see if she was okay. These people had a clear enough view of the world to understand how seriously my wife's fooling around ought to be taken.

Who knows why it came upon her and why it departed? Serotonin, hormones, neurons, the light. Childhood, puberty, childbirth, the heavy passing of time. All explanations are cliché, as is the assertion that there can finally be no explanation. In the end I can only try to make sense of my wife's depression and the death of David Foster Wallace on my own terms, for my own purposes; to grasp or articulate to myself what my fiction has been saying to the world all along.

The world, like our heads, was meant to be escaped from. They are prisons, world and head alike. "I guess a big part of serious fiction's purpose," Wallace once told an interviewer, "is to give the reader, who like all of us is sort of marooned in her own skull, to give her imaginative access to other selves." The purpose or the blessing of that kind of access—which I have often thought of and characterized by means of the word *escape*—is ultimately to increase our sense of shared experience, of shared suffering, rapture, nostalgia, or disgust, with our fellow humans, whose thoughts and emotions are otherwise locked away. And yet that gift of access, for all its marvelous power to console the lonely and to dislodge the complacent, is a kind of trick, an act of Houdiniesque illusion. When the vision fades and the colored smoke disperses, we are left alone and marooned again in our skulls with nothing but our longing for connection. That longing drives writers and readers to seek the high, small window leading out, to lower the makeshift ropes of knotted bedsheet that stories and literature afford, and make a break for it. When that window can't be found, or will no longer serve, or when it inevitably turns out to be only paint on the unchanging, impenetrable backdrop of our heads, small wonder if the longing seeks another, surer means of egress.

Radio Silence

Not long before it went off the air forever, KFRC-FM switched its format to Greatest Hits of the '70s and '80s, a change that left me feeling oddly freaked. Before the switch, KFRC had been a standard oldies station playing pop, rock, and soul hits spanning the era from the middle to late 1950s to the middle 1970s, roughly from Elvis Presley and Chuck Berry to the O'Jays and *Rumours*-era Fleetwood Mac. But the core of the playlist was pure sixties: the British Invasion and Motown, bookended by the Four Seasons and Sly Stone. The switch in format had been covered in the local press, but somehow I had missed it. The change itself, the disproportionate share suddenly given over to music of the seventies, was subtle enough to elude me for a little while. And then one day I realized that KFRC was playing a song by Phil Collins, and I felt a weird minor grief.

The old format hadn't offered a revelatory or even, I suppose, very interesting playlist. If you listened to KFRC a lot—and I still listen to broadcast music on a conventional radio all the time, every day, in my car and in my house—you tended to hear the same two or three hundred songs over and over and over. They played not the big hits but the famous hits, aural monuments such as Buffalo Springfield's "For What It's Worth" and Marvin Gaye's version of "I Heard It Through the Grapevine," tracks that are no longer even really songs at all so much as logos of the decade that produced them. The station rarely played wondrous freaks of the charts (say, "Something in the Air," by Thunderclap Newman, which reached No. 37), minor hits such as the Box Tops' "Soul Deep" (No. 18), or sixties hits by groups like the Who, more likely to be encountered on stations with a classic-rock format. Certain tracks seemed to fall randomly into intense rotation, and you would hear the Blues Image's "Ride Captain Ride" (a fine song, I hasten to add, with excellent support from future Iron Butterfly guitarist Mike Pinera) almost every day for months on end, often at roughly the same time of day.

It's hard to see why I should have found the format switch so disturbing. I own far more great pop music of the sixties (and of the seventies, for that matter) than KFRC ever played, and thanks to MP3s and my iPod, I can listen to it whenever and wherever I want to. What difference does it make if there's nowhere on the FM dial to hear Herman's Hermits sing "I'm Into Something Good"? There. Three mouse clicks and I'm listening to Peter Noone. Two more clicks and I'm listening to the superior pure-British pop stylings of minor geniuses the Honeybus, who never charted in the U.S. and may never have been heard on any radio station here ever. Big deal. So why, on the day when I dialed in to 99.7 and heard

"Sussudio" and had the creeping realization that the shift had taken place weeks ago without my ever quite noticing, did I feel that vertiginous despair?

I'm old. That was my first thought. I'm so old that a hit song from a year when I was already in graduate school now qualifies as an oldie. But that wasn't really the source of my unease. The length of time required to coat a hit song with a layer of oldie dust has always been breathtakingly short. When George Lucas's *American Graffiti* came out in 1973, the oldest number on its sound track was Bill Haley and the Comets' "(We're Gonna) Rock Around the Clock," and that song sounded utterly ancient to my nine-year-old ears. Every song featured in American Graffiti—as with the fashions, the hair, the automotive styles, the whole world the movie depicted—felt as distant, as removed from me as Laurel and Hardy or the Andrews Sisters, though in fact it was set only ten years before its release. There may be no span of years longer than that which separates your parents' youth from your own. I heard Prince's "Let's Go Crazy" the other day, and I could easily imagine, could feel, just how remote the world of that song and *Purple Rain* (about as distant from my eight-year-old as Bill Haley was from me) must sound and look to a kid today.

My mother loved *American Graffiti*, and it was in her car, in her memories, and with her generation (she was born in 1942) that I first encountered the concept of the golden oldie. My mother liked to listen to a D.C. station, WMOD ("Washington's Goldmine"). The playlist—as I dimly recall—derived entirely from the era bracketed by Big Joe Turner and Lesley Gore: doo-wop, rockabilly, girl groups, surf music, pre-Motown soul, novelty weepers like "Tell Laura I Love Her," country hits like Carl Smith's "There She Goes," and anything that constituted what was then known as classic rock and roll. "Runaround Sue," by Dion & the Belmonts (1961), was my mother's all-time favorite. We used to hear it sometimes on WMOD, and she always got a certain look when it came on, something between surprise and reverie.

All those songs and, even more, their familiarity and evident importance to my mother—the associations and memories they stirred, the good feelings they engendered—came to mean something to me. Their lyrics, their instrumentation, the outmoded crooning or falsettos of their vocalists, their monaural shimmer, became part of my understanding of the era that had produced them, and of my understanding of my mother, and of the way she saw and talked about her life. Most important, they alerted me to the mysterious power of the chance interaction between radio and memory.

My earliest memory not supported or supplanted by a photograph is of a song on the radio. I was with my mother in some kind of doctor's office in downtown Phoenix (and therefore not yet four years old). We were downtown, because in the song that was playing on the radio in the doctor's office, a lady was singing about what a great thing it was to go downtown, where the lights were much brighter and you could forget all your cares. *Things will be great*, this lady promised, *when you're downtown.* I looked around. I remember a fearsome nurse in white stockings, glass jars with chrome lids, a maternal promise of lunch in a restaurant after the appointment. I think I was just old enough to understand that there was and could be no direct connection between my physical whereabouts and the place referred to by the song that I was hearing on the radio. It was coincidence. I knew that. But that fortuity invested the moment with a shock and a magic that reverberated down the next forty years. When I hear Petula Clark on the radio now, if the circumstances are right—the station AM, the speakers tinny, the volume low—I feel this wave of something old and powerful flowing through my chest and my belly, a bodily remembering of that crucial early-childhood compound of anxiety and the promise of a treat.

Sometimes a song happens to come on the radio and imbue a moment that way, with its aptness. More often there is no obvious thematic connection between a song on the radio and the memory that it somehow or other comes to preserve, between the iridescent bubble of the music and the air of the past that it randomly traps. It's simply the magic of an accidental conjunction, a flitting moment and the resin drop of a pop song transformed by luck and alchemy into amber. The radiant shins of a girl named Jennifer Dagenais, for example, as she oiled herself with Bain de Soleil at the Phelps Luck swimming pool in the summer of 1978 are retained in the opening riff of "Hold the Line" by Toto. The Megginsons, and my fondness for them, and the vinegar smell of a bushel of apples we had just picked at Sewell's Orchard, and all of us crammed into their rattletrap orange VW Beetle, is restored to me for some reason by a forgotten Three Dog Night hit, "The Show Must Go On" (1974).

No medium is as sensuously evocative of the past as radio. No other medium deploys that shocking full-immersion power of random remembrance. But for the power to have its maximum impact, the process of remembering has to be random at both ends. Joe Jackson's "Is She Really Going Out with Him?" is playing over the PA in a Gap store at the Mall in Columbia on an unremarkable afternoon when you're sixteen, and then one day you're forty and driving to get your kid from nursery school and the song comes on, and there in your minivan you can smell the chlorine from the mall's fountain, and hear your best friend telling you about Pauline Kael's review of *Last Tango in Paris* as reprinted in *Reeling*, and see the vast blue wall of denim before you, and remember the world in which Bill Murray was God and Jimmy Carter was president and in which, at the Gap, they sold nothing but Levi's. The song has to take you by surprise, catch you when your guard is down, when you aren't expecting it—ideally, when you aren't even listening to the radio at all. A bright little piece of your life passes you by in a car with the windows rolled down, wells up in the pain-relief aisle of a Rite-Aid. That kind of chance encounter can't happen as readily on an iPod you've programmed yourself.

The sense of mourning I felt when I realized that KFRC had changed its format was not over the music—the music is all there, at ninety-nine cents a download—but over this sudden sealing off, as if by avalanche or detonation, of an entire network of tunnels, secret passageways, into the past. Into history as an everyday thing that happens between visits to the doctor and rides home from picking apples. That is, I was suffering from a sudden loss of memory. Most of my own pop history was still well represented on the updated KFRC playlist. But the process of radio oblivion is inexorable and steady. Just as I didn't notice at first when a huge swath of the 1960s pop charts disappeared from the KFRC playlist, so I hadn't noticed when the hits of the fifties had disappeared—exiled, I suppose, to one of those forlorn AM stations that used to play only Perry Como and Rosemary Clooney and Dick Haymes, the last stop before those songs disappear entirely from the landscape of everyday memory, along with the people whose history they preserve, in luminous fragments. And now WBIG, the station that succeeded WMOD as the home of oldies in Washington, D.C., has modified its format, as did New York's storied WCBS before that, and KFRC is off the air, shriveled down to a tiny streaming audio link on the KCBS Web site. "The audience is getting older," explained the Clear Channel executive responsible for the change in programming at WBIG, "and going away." Now I know how I will know when I am gone.

Normal Time

We've had a run of crazy stuff going on around here lately, culminating (for the moment) with global economic collapse and my mother-in-law's suffering an injury that looks as if it may permanently alter the contour and quality of her life, as well as the whole family's—a pair of calamities that followed on a series of unpleasant surprises, diagnoses, minor crises, the dog undergoing a "spinal stroke," professional setbacks, sorrows in the second grade, the loss or destruction of many objects of value, a brutal twenty-month-long presidential campaign, and all the usual, unusual alarums and disruptions that result when six people and a Bernese mountain dog, requiring various mental, emotional, and physical accommodations, therapies, and treatments, conduct an ongoing experiment in measuring mutual interference in one another's reality distortion fields by sharing a house in Berkeley, California, a place that may, at any moment—which will, given the way things have been going lately—be destroyed by a massive once-a-millennium earthquake, or by a raging October wildfire, or by the fire that immediately follows the earthquake. And when I say *lately*, I'm using the term very loosely. This shit has been going on around here for years.

The thing is, we are six lucky people (and a dog), and all our needs and desires are amply met. We have set up the household to run smoothly when possible and to recover quickly when smooth is not an option. The children do their chores and their homework, the adults our work as spouses, parents, and writers, and if you took a sample of any random hour any day, if you employed some human calculus to arrest our progress, to ascertain our state at any given instant, you would find contentment with one another's company, love and respect, a fruitful exchange of ideas, compulsive storytelling, joking around, even the odd outbreak of peace and quiet. But since this thing with my poor mother-in-law (broken femur, shattered wrist), I've been sitting here trying to figure out how long it has been since the days around here have been normal. Steady. Routine. Productive. Neither beset nor fraught nor teetering on some brink of disaster, free of emergency and crisis. I spend a lot of time thinking about, wishing for, working to arrange and to render inevitable, the return to our lives of Normal Time. And yet in trying to work my way back to the last golden era, I find myself casting my memory so far that the exercise begins to call into the question the very idea—an idea, by the way, that forms the basis of my understanding of our family life, here on our notional seam between the fault line and the burn zone—that there has ever been such a time. It turns out that the whole thing may be a delusion.

Like everyone—I hope—I suffer from a number of delusions, many of them apparently ineradicable. There are the geographical delusions. When I am in Pittsburgh or Paris, for example, I can never prevent myself from thinking of the point where the Allegheny, Monongahela, and Ohio conjoin as facing eastward, or of the Left Bank as extending to the north of Notre-Dame. Most of my delusions of longest standing have to do (such is my legacy as a human being) with the acuity of my judgment, of my memory, and of my insight into the hearts of others. But the worst and most wondrous of the delusions that plague me tend to take the form, like this idea of Normal Time, of vague but unquestioned certainties about the nature and course of my life.

Here's an example: I am forty-five years old. By even the most conservative estimate, it has been nearly a quarter of a century since I climbed eagerly aboard this one-way rocket to Death in Adulthood and left the planet of my childhood forever in my starry wake. I know this. My grandparents, my boyhood bedroom furniture, a miniature schnauzer of admirable character named Fritz, the dazed and goofy splendor of bicentennial America: I will never see any of those or a million other things again. And yet always lurking somewhere in the back of my mind is the unshakable, even foundational knowledge—for which certainty is too conscious a term—that at some unspecified future date, by unspecified means, I will return to those people and to those locales. That I am going back.

No, that's false. The delusion is not really that I believe or trust that I will be returning one day to the planet of childhood; it's that the world I left behind so long ago is still there, somewhere, to be returned to; that it continues to exist, sideburns, Evel Knievel, Spiro T. Agnew, and all, like some alternate-time-line Krypton that never exploded, just on the other side of the phantom-zone barrier that any determined superman would know how to pierce. When I watch a film or a television show from the period and see again the workingmen wearing short-sleeved shirts with neck-ties, or the great wide slabs of Detroit automobiles, or the blue mailboxes with the red tops, or when I happen to hear from some random radio the DeFranco Family singing "Heartbeat (It's a Love Beat)," I do not think merely, *Oh, that's right, I remember that* or the more pathetic *I wish I could go back there again*. What I feel is something more like gratitude, a sense of relief, the way you feel when you wake from a dream in which your beloved has died, and the world is grief and winter, and then you find her warm and snoring in the bed beside you.

But even that delusion pales beside this mad hankering, this utopian or millenarian yearning for the coming days of Normal Time, of time to spare, of time in plenty. Time not just for work and reflection and unhurried lovemaking but for all kinds of fine and tiny things. Time to learn German. Time to print out the digital photos and reorganize the albums. Time to lavish on my younger children as I seem to have lavished it on their older siblings (though back then I thought there was never enough time for anything). Time for regular lunches with my mother. Time to get deep into a baseball season again, to linger over the box scores in the morning, to watch a meaningless game between teams I don't care about, just out of fondness for the game. Time to write the short stories I used to fling like Frisbees out into the blue, the libretto for an opera of *The Long Goodbye*, an annotated version of my failed, never-completed novel *Fountain City*. Time simply to stretch out, to play with, to dandle and dilate and waste with my children and my wife.

Instead it's just, as Arnold Toynbee or Henry Ford or Dr. McCoy used to say of history, one damn thing after another, and often several damn things at the same time, overlapping swaths of color on the digital calendar, conflicts and cancellations, two tasks half-done badly where one might have been pulled off in style. There is never, in the words of Irish poet Tom Paulin, any "long lulled pause / before history happens." Only days after my wife and I guided our last baby into kindergarten, we began preparing in earnest to send our half-grown woman off to high school next fall; in the interval, the stock market crashed and my mother-in-law fell down a flight of stairs. There is no Normal Time, or rather, this is it, with all its accidents and discontinuities. With a breathtaking sequence, your last child leaves home, gets married, has children, and then you fall and break your leg, and the next thing you know, you're approaching the point at which space curves back on itself or doesn't. The end, unless the end, too, is a delusion. After that, either way, there is no time at all, and you're never going back again.

Xmas

I was walking past a public elementary school off Solano Avenue a few weeks ago and noticed, hanging over its entrance, a large paper banner decorated in orange and black, featuring a motif of jack-o'-lanterns and scarecrows and proclaiming the imminent observation by its students of the school's annual Harvest Festival at the end of October. The sign, like the other elements of decor hung from the gates of the schoolyard, said nothing about Halloween. There was no imagery of ghosts, bats, witches, haunted houses, etc., but I noticed that aside from the pumpkins and the scarecrows, there was nothing in the way of agricultural or other harvesttime imagery, either—no haystacks or, I don't know, ripened ears of maize, cornucopias, sickles, threshing machines, ritual stonings. Apart from the gardens in its backyards—lavish as many of those are—and the bounty of hydroponic plantations in its closets and basements, Berkeley, California, has, as far as I know, no harvest to be observed. I wondered whose sensibilities were being respected by this absurd bit of subterfuge or, if you prefer, cultural sensitivity. Perhaps those of evangelical Christians who have been known to object to the historical association of the eve of All Saints' Day with witches, devils, and other characters one would have imagined might fall beneath the contempt of a truly effective personal savior, at least when depicted in crepe paper, latex, and cake frosting. Or maybe it was, paradoxically, non-Christians whose feelings were being respected, given the connection between Halloween and the ancient Catholic feast of All Hallows. Or maybe the decision to rebrand and denature Halloween had been made out of respect for, though without recourse to any observable facts about or even a passing knowledge of, the feelings of small children. But mostly, I wondered, *Who the hell do the people who authorized that sign and that "festival" think they're kidding?*

I'm not saying that school districts—or anybody else, for that matter—ought to go around scaring people without their consent, or that disrespecting people's feelings ought to be any public institution's official policy, though I think I could make an argument for the latter in certain cases, such as that of people who see grave moral danger in an eight-year-old wearing a bedsheet. I don't think public schools should impose Christian worship on anybody, least of all Christians. I don't want my children taught that it's all right to persecute or demean others for their beliefs or, for that matter, that on October 31 the souls of the damned rise up from their graves to go carousing with the Prince of Evil. But if had a choice, I might pick either of those over teaching them that it's our unavoidable lot as modern humans to dwell everlastingly, wearing an eternal smirk of knowingness, in bullshit.

The same thing goes for Christmas and the by now ubiquitous school holiday or winter pageant. I am a liberal agnostic empiricist, proud to be a semi-observant, bacon-eating Jew, and I have only contempt for the intolerance, ignorance, anti-intellectualism, self-deception, implicit violence, and misogyny that underlie religious fundamentalism of every flavor, from bearded to clean-cut. But I'm all for putting the Christ back in Christmas, and not only in the hope, doubtless in vain, that it might shut a few evangelical Christians up. It pains me to say it, but the people who argue that it's dishonest to equate Christmas, Hanukkah, and Kwanzaa are, at least in this instance, and with very little in the way of percentage gain in their own overall level of honesty or correctness, correct. I like to eat latkes as much as the next Jew, and candlelight is lovely, but the glorification of Hanukkah by American Jews is another example of voluntary group self-deception. It's an exercise in collective bad faith in which everyone agrees to ignore what everyone knows to be true: that Hanukkah is a pissant holiday elevated beyond its station and intrinsic meaning for the gratification of toy manufacturers, greeting-card companies, and the makers of chocolate coins wrapped in gold foil, in an effort to battle the cultural stranglehold of Christmas, an effort that has never been and never will be successful, if only because Hanukkah songs are so painfully lame. As for Kwanzaa, I can't say for sure, but I see no compelling reason to give it the benefit of the doubt. Christmas is a big deal, a much bigger deal than Hanukkah or Kwanzaa or any other Christian holiday, for that matter, apart from Easter. So, fine, let's put the Christ back in it or get rid of Christmas entirely.

Either way, let's do it honestly, which, if we are fundamentalists, means throwing out Santa Claus, candy canes, and mistletoe, not to mention decorated trees, light-up life-size plastic reindeer, and the entire Christmas economy itself.

Thank God, though, we are not fundamentalists. And maybe there's a way we can keep Christmas, Christ and all, and still respect and acknowledge both the traditions of non-Christians and the First Amendment of the Constitution. Because I would kind of hate to lose Christmas, a holiday that—as with poor old Jesus Himself—I've always been rather fond of.

In my family, the yearly colonization of Jews by Christmas produced a kind of pidgin holiday free of adjectives and ritual angst. The Feast of the Nativity of the Blessed Savior, Jesus Christ, the King of the World, born amid portents and miracles in the manger with the talking animals and the little drummer boy, was put through an extremely fine sieve, leaving only a residue: stockings over the fireplace personalized with Elmer's glue and glitter, a half-gallon of eggnog in the refrigerator, and a set menu of animated television shows (A Charlie Brown Christmas, The Year Without a Santa Claus, and the parable of Whoville). There was a stocking for the dog, too, in which, on Christmas morning, he would find a dog biscuit just like every other dog biscuit he had ever been given but which he would nonetheless greet with a gratifying show of holiday spirit. We didn't have a mantel to hang our stockings from, mantels having fallen out of fashion by then, so we hung them on the iron utensil hooks with the poker and the shovel and the tongs. To this thin Yuletide residue we then added a few syncretistic customs of our people. We went to the movies with a bagful of chocolate Santas, having ensured beforehand that they were solid and not hollow. We went for a walk in our gloves and scarves, admiring the doorways and windows of our gentile neighbors' houses, crayoned in lights against the evening, with the hasty squiggle of a tree or a hedge in front. Most crucial, we ate dinner at a Chinese restaurant. And even though we ate dinner at the very same Chinese restaurant at least twice a month, the Christmas meal seemed more leisurely, and the traditional pupu platter, with its central flickering brazier of heatless comedy fire, lent a festive suggestion of bounty and esoteric rites. The whole day was like that, a bright flame that did not burn, a holiday without gravity or meaning or claim on our memories, a lost day when the stores closed, the roads emptied, people stayed inside their houses, and the world was briefly left to Jews like us to do with as we pleased.

Still, there were, every year, strange face-to-face encounters with the conquering holiday that left me feeling obscurely moved. Take that *Peanuts* TV special, for example. At its climax, Linus Van Pelt, the character with whom I most strongly identified, saved the day by reminding everyone, in the lean, poignant language of the King James Bible, of the reason for the ornaments and pageants and teriyaki-pineapple chunks on bamboo skewers. It never occurred to me to wonder whether any of it could possibly be true. The idea that Jesus Christ was the Son of God, that He was the Messiah, that if you did not believe in Him you would go to hell, and so forth, these ideas were even more insubstantial to me then than they are now, when my learning to doubt everything has created a condition strongly akin to that of fierce belief. But all the same, there was something profoundly touching in Linus's voice when he spoke those words, particularly when he got to the part where the angel of the Lord appeared to the shepherds "and they were sore afraid." There was nothing about the story in itself that was any more powerful or moving or true than the stories over on our side of the Bible, but it was a story fixed upon, so determinedly and exhaustively, by all my favorite forms of popular media, from comic strips to sitcoms to the radio playing "Jingle Bell Rock," a story repeated so often that I could not help but respond on some deep level to its appeal, to its promises of answered prayers and brotherhood and home.

I don't see anything wrong with that; *A Charlie Brown Christmas* didn't convert me, or threaten me, or imperil my ties to Judaism. What it did was educate me. But then the antidote to any kind of bullshit, bad faith, hypocrisy, or cant, whether offered in the name of Jesus or of multiculturalism, is always education. I still know that chapter and verse of the Gospel of Luke by heart, and no amount of subsequent disillusionment with the behavior of self-described Christians, or with the ongoing progressive commercialization that in 1965 had already broken Charlie Brown's heart, has robbed the central miracle of Christianity of its power to move me the way any truly great story can.

My own children have attended a private school administered under the auspices of the Episcopal Church. Every year, as part of the school's annual Christmas pageant, the second-graders put on a Nativity play, just like the Peanuts kids. They dress as sheep, wise men, Joseph, Mary, angels of the Lord—my daughter wore a halo, and my son carried a shepherd's crook. The story is presented straight, in the language of the gospels, with the sole nods to multiculturalism being a running translation into Spanish provided by their schoolmates and musical accompaniment by the choir singing Nativity-related carols from around the world. During the first part of the program, there are usually a couple of Hanukkah songs and a nod to Kwanzaa. But there is no Hanukkah play, no reenactment of the miracle of the oil or even, for that matter, any mention of the Maccabees at all.

There are a fair number of Jewish kids at the school, and I know that sitting through the annual recounting of the birth of Jesus—an event that, however opportune for Christians, has brought millennia of suffering and persecution to Jews—makes many of their parents uncomfortable. Even more than the Friday chapels (at which the kids are admittedly as likely to hear about Ramadan, César Chávez, Yom Kippur, or recycling as they are about the life of, say, St. Brigid), the Nativity play seems to quicken all their anxieties about sending their little Jews to an ecumenical and progressive but unabashedly Christian school.

Not me. I love hearing the story of Jesus' birth, and I always have, just as I have always loved hearing about the births of Moses, King Arthur, Hercules, John Henry, and the Peach Boy of Japanese folklore. Like all stories of miraculous births, the Nativity is the story of a great promise being made to the world. In the case of Christ, that promise, while unredeemed, has led demonstrably to the making of the world we live in, and if the subsequent years have brought as much disgrace as glory to those who have accepted or claimed to accept the promise of Jesus' birth, I don't think it does anyone any harm to hear the promise itself: a statement of hope, forgiveness, and love among all the people of the world, repeated by a bunch of little kids dressed up in kingly turbans and cottony fleece. On the contrary, it breaks my heart every time.

Sure, it's a lie—if there was a Jesus, chances are He wasn't born under anything resembling the circumstances narrated by St. Luke, Linus, or the second grade at St. Paul's. But unlike banning ghosts and witches from Halloween or adding a light splash of latke to the winter pageant, it's a lie that tells the truth: about the hope and the promise that ought to attend the birth of every child, however mean or difficult the conditions of that birth and however disadvantaged and persecuted that child's people; about the dangerous and woefully unredeemed state of the world and the potential that all children have to redeem it, or else perishing therein like the innocents doomed by Herod for the crime of having been born.

There is no use pretending that Christmas is not beautiful, or that it can be finessed away or filed down to an innocuous nub by the rasp of cultural sensitivity. Changing the name of Halloween to the Harvest Festival changes nothing; it just adds another slug to the treasury of counterfeits out of which we pay our children's fare through the world. Like all of us, my kids ought to hear the truth about Christianity, a truth that is built, like all human truths, on a story woven of wishes, possibilities, and lies. They need to be taught to judge the followers of Jesus as we all must be judged, and taught to judge on our own terms, by our own claims and asseverations, by the promises we hold out to the world, and by the betrayal of those promises. Unless we hear the story, the lie, in all its power, we will never fully understand the truth of it, nor how far short all of us—including those who most fervently profess that truth—fall.

The Amateur Family

At the museum we handed over our coats to a pleasant young man with an English accent, and something about us, my children and me, stunned him. His eyes widened and his mouth fell open; he looked as if he had been, as I believe his countrymen would put it, gob-smacked.

The source of his astonishment turned out to be, of all things, the design silkscreened on my older son's T-shirt. The young Brit marveled at it, then at my son, then turned to me, helpless, hoping for an explanation of this impossible thing. "Is that—is that a *Dalek?*" he said.

But that was not what he wanted to ask us; he knew the answer to the question. Of *course* it was a Dalek—one of those mobile armored shells, shaped roughly like traffic cones, studded at their base with convex dots and tricked out at the rounded tip with a couple of death-dealing wands (one of them resembling suspiciously a toilet plunger); metal husks whose kernels are the pulpy, sluglike, extremely irritable former inhabitants of the planet Skaro, embarked since 1964 on a tireless mission to conquer the universe of the classic British television program *Doctor Who*. What the young Englishman at the Smithsonian really wanted to ask was *What the hell do you people know from Daleks?* Here he was in America, a land and a television market in which *Doctor Who* had never taken off; the Daleks, shrill, priggish, occasionally rather hysterical cybernetic staples of the nightmares of British children for forty-five years, were supposed to be far away, across the sea, gone forever—canceled, even, along with the original program, in 1989.

"There's a new show," I said. "A new *Doctor Who*."

"*Is* there?"

My children and I looked at one another, marveling ourselves. Poor, sad little Englishman in Washington, so far from home. *He didn't know!*

"It's on Sci-Fi Network," my older daughter explained. At the moment, she was not wearing her Time Lord T-shirt (the show's eponymous doctor hails from Gallifrey, homeworld of the Time Lords). "And BBC America and PBS. Or you can just download them from iTunes."

"I have a Cybermen T-shirt," my youngest son put in, referring to the less perfectly terrifying yet still awesome-looking second-banana metal nemeses of the Doctor. "I wore it yesterday. But I threw up on it on the plane."

"And I have one with K-9," said my younger daughter. During the 1970s run of the show, K-9 was a robot dog who—but no, perhaps we had better not get into K-9.

"It's a pretty good show," I said, but I knew that my tone and my posture and the wild fannish tenor of my voice were saying *It's the greatest show ever in the history of television.*

As we began to engulf him in the intensity of our passion for *Doctor Who*, a different light came into the young man's face, less bewildered, a light of tolerant understanding. He took our coats, his face animated by the faint hint of a smirk. He had us now. We were a family of geeks.

"*Ex-ter-minate*," we said in fluent Dalek.

I don't own a *Doctor Who* T-shirt, but if I did, like my children, I most certainly would have so informed the young Englishman taking our coats. Indeed, I would not have been able to prevent myself from doing so; I suppose I *am* a geek, the geek matrix of four bright geek spawn. And if you aren't watching and loving the glorious new BBC incarnation of *Doctor Who*, geeking out on the mythos of Daleks and Time Lords and Cybermen, swooning to the polysexual heroics of Captain Jack Harkness, aching over the quantum transdimensional heartache of Rose Tyler, and granting yourself the supreme and steady pleasure of watching the dazzling Scottish actor David Tennant go about the business of being the tenth man to embody the time-and-space traveling Doctor on television since the show's debut in 1963, then I pity you with the especial harsh pity of the geek.

I had always hoped and worked with patience and care—offering running seminars in Vulcan physiology, Jon Anderson lyrics, the history of the Marvel Universe—to have geeky children, though the term *geek*, like its common synonym *nerd*, is woefully imprecise, with connotations of physical awkwardness, high-water trousers, loserhood, emotional retardation, etc. *Geek* carries as well the additional unfortunate echo of sideshow freaks orally decapitating chickens. *Fan* is more accurate, I suppose, but it spends too much time hanging around the sports page and ESPN, and anyway, the word (even with its fanspeak plural, *fen*) is a clipped form of the pejorative *fanatic*, with all its connotations of narrowness, intolerance, unreason, a condemnatory fervor. *Fanboy* gets tossed around a lot these days, but two of my children are female, and *fanchild* is not a word, and the term was originally coined to describe and deprecate a kind of mindless, by-the-greasy-handful consumption of popular culture, uncritical, automatic, halfway to *zombie*.

Perhaps there is no perfect word for the kind of people I have raised my children to be: a word that encompasses obsessive scholarship, passionate curiosity, curatorial tenderness, and an irrepressible desire to join in the game, to inhabit in some manner—through writing, drawing, dressing up, or endless conversational riffing and Talmudic debate—the world of the endlessly inviting, endlessly inhabitable work of popular art. The closest I have ever come for myself is *amateur*, in all the original best senses of the word: a lover; a devotee; a person driven by passion and obsession to do it—to explore the imaginary world—oneself. And if we must accept the inevitable connotation of hopeless ineptitude that *amateur* carries, then at least let us stipulate that we shall be hopeless and inept like Max Fischer, the hero of Wes Anderson's *Rushmore*: in the most passionate, heedless, and whole-hearted way.

I was that kind of a fanchild—a passionate amateur—I have grown up to be that kind of man, and my writing, straight up to my most recent novel, represents an ongoing effort to write myself into the worlds and the narratives, from those of Conan Doyle and Fritz Leiber to those of F. Scott Fitzgerald and Gabriel García Márquez, that I grew up longing to inhabit. As a child, I was lucky enough to have a father who inculcated in me a love of *Star Trek*, Japanese monster movies, the Marx Brothers, comic books, and the like. I suppose we constituted a fan club of two. But when I was twelve years old, my parents divorced, and my father moved far away, leaving me to inhabit above all else, loving it or not, a world characterized chiefly by its immense solitude. I could not drive, and suburban Maryland was no white-hot center of fandom. I had no access to the world of self-published APAs and fanzines that preceded (and helped to shape the culture of) the Internet. My younger brother was born without the mutated fanboy protein, utterly uninterested in the question of whether Spock's human mother had been won through the ritual combat of the Pon Farr or whether the Atlantis of Superman's mermaid girlfriend, Lori Lemaris, was the same as Aquaman's Atlantis. I was left alone, a fan club of one, and perhaps that was not unusual, because solitude is the portion of every geek, nerd, or fanboy, and I was kind of an amateur of solitude, too.

It is only recently, as I and my children (and lately, even their mother) have plunged into the exceptionally rich, dense, and time-layered world of *Doctor Who* fandom, that I've begun to understand the accidental gift that I (and she) have given our four little ama-teurs, geeking out in the back of the minivan over, let's say, the exact nature of the plunderous, flatulent Slitheen family of extraterrestrials, or the intricate, paradoxical mystery of the Time War that supposedly wiped out all the Daleks and all the Time Lords except for the Doctor: We have given them one another.

For in playing, or writing, or drawing, or simply talking oneself deep into the world of a popular artwork that invites the regard of the amateur, the fan, one is seeking above all to *connect*, not only with the world of the show, comic book, or film but with the encircling, embracing metaworld of all those who love it as much as you do. As a kid, I always seemed to have trouble with that aspect of the art of being a fan; for many, many years after my father left home, I found it difficult to reach out and find other people with whom I could construct a shared universe of enthusiasm. But my kids have one another, four little Whoheads in cryptic T-shirts that only they and a random British dude understand.

And of course they have me, and—of course—I have them. Together we have spent hours not only watching and talking about the show but drawing our own versions of putative Eleventh and Twelfth and Twenty-Seventh Doctors, drawing pictures of Daleks and Cybermen and of the Tardis, the Doctor's time-and-space machine, disguised as a vintage wooden phone booth. We have made Tardises and Daleks out of Lego bricks and have worked out our own scenarios for the resurrection of the unfortunate dimension-lost Rose Tyler.

The greatest, most essential creation of fandom is fandom itself, and maybe all along, part of my desire to have so many children was the longing for a fan club to belong to, for imaginative fellowship, for the society of passionate amateurs like me. In my children, I have found a band of companions—like the companions, Rose Tyler among them, who have always accompanied the Doctor on his adventures—as surely as they have found companions in one another.

Every one of the Doctor's human companions comes to learn, eventually, the hard truth: Sooner or later, the adventure will cease. The Doctor will leave them behind, abandon them, move on to a new incarnation, a new season, a new companion; this melancholy fate lends a strange and mournful gravity to a show that is otherwise unfailingly jaunty, even when it is telling stories that are spooky, romantic, or profound. My own dear Doctor lost track of me on the Planet of the Seventies, and since then he and I never have quite found our way home. In the hands, minds, and geekish chatter of my children, I have found again that long-lost, long-desired connection. Each of us stands ready, at any moment, to talk *Who*, to riff and spin and sketch out new contours for the world we collectively inhabit, creating and endlessly re-creating the fandom that is our family.

Maybe all families are a kind of fandom, an endlessly elaborated, endlessly disputed, endlessly reconfigured set of commentaries, extrapolations, and variations generated by passionate amateurs on the primal text of the parents' love for each other. Sometimes the original program is canceled by death or separation; sometimes, as with *Doctor Who*, it endures and flourishes for decades. And maybe love, mortality, and loss, and all the children and mythologies and sorrows they engender, make passionate amateurs—nerds, geeks, and fanboys—of us all.

[X]

CUE THE MICKEY KATZ

Daughter of the Commandment

My oldest child became a bat mitzvah in an afternoon Sabbath service. She read from the Torah in flawless Hebrew, taught us something about what she had just read in poignant English, and was blessed by a woman of readily apparent holiness. And then she was on her way: a daughter of the Commandments.

Now, everyone knows—sorry, Maimonides—that there really is only one Commandment and that, sooner or later, we all obey it. Toward the end of every Sabbath service, those in mourning or observing the anniversary of a parent's death rise for the ancient Kaddish, and as the parent of that day's bar or bat mitzvah, you can sit there beaming, proud, filled with love and knowing—knowing—that if you have done your job properly, it will not be long before your child will be getting up from a pew somewhere to take note in Aramaic of your own utter absence from the world.

This poignance, this sense of the sweet and brutal passage of time, is a key part of what one is supposed to feel at weddings and bar mitzvahs. These ceremonies break your heart; they are de-signed, as A. B. Giamatti wrote of baseball, to break your heart. Autumnal thoughts are inevitable as you watch your child lay a first tentative foot on that high scrabbly hillside and look up, shading her eyes from the dazzle, toward the rest of her life. I can remember being thirteen and feeling stifled, half drowned, by the corniness of it any time some aunt at the piano took up the minor notes of "Sunrise, Sunset" and all the adults wiped their eyes and wondered where my infancy and their youth and all the days had gone. But you know what? I spent hours putting together an iTunes playlist for us to dance to at the reception after the ser-vice, soliciting suggestions via e-mail from a team of party-mix experts, black-belt Snoopy-style dancers, and former part-time semiprofessional soi-disant DJs, a process that resulted in a selec-tion of tracks glorious and replete and nearly perfect, with Prince ("Kiss"), New Order ("Bizarre Love Triangle"), and L.T.D. ("Every Time I Turn Around, Back In Love Again"), and yet the song that reached right down to the very core of me was the final tune of the evening, the only tune you need, Mickey Katz's perfect, wordless one minute forty-eight second dance-band version of, God help me, "Sunrise, Sunset."

So, all right, swiftly fly the years, I get it. What a tiresome, empty observation, finally, when compared to *You don't have to watch Dynasty to have an attitude* or *Every time I see you falling / I get down on my knees and pray.* Anyway, apart from that minute and forty-eight seconds of melancholy bliss with Katz and his clari-net, that's not what I found myself thinking about yesterday: She is young and strong, and I am graying, have acid reflux, and my neck hurts, and soon I am going to be dead, true though all of those statements may be. First of all, I feel that I am in the prime of my life. I have never understood more (though still very few) of life's mysteries than I do now, or trusted my instincts to a greater degree, or written better sentences than the ones I find myself writing sometimes these days. In spite of the creaky neck and the occasional needle of fire in my belly, my bones, joints, and organs remain more or less in good working order. Recently, I was reading the latest, last Nathan Zuckerman novel, and I felt nearly as distant from its protagonist's physical decline and preoccupation with onrushing mortality as I might have twenty years ago.

It's not that I never find entertaining the cheery notion, for example, that my life is quite probably at least half over. That idea can be an instructive, and I don't doubt that most of us benefit from thoughtfully confronting our mortality on a regular basis. But in the end, memento mori is only going to get you so far, and as a buzzkill at parties, it's second only to breaking out pictures of your kid's head coming out of your wife's vagina.

And looking at my fine half-grown daughter as she led the afternoon service, her slender neck arched like a feat of engineering, her alto steady, clear, and shining like the silver pointer that she clasped in her hand as it traced the path of the Hebrew letters on the parchment before her, I found myself considering not time's passage but its unfathomable stillness, its immobility, the great universal fiction that there is such a thing as time. Your children's childhoods as you watch them unscroll are always indexed to your own, visibly and invisibly, their incidents and episodes, pleasures, and calamities snarled with your own. Your childhood, or your memory of it, is present in every moment of theirs, answering it and prefiguring it and shadowing it like a continuo. And then every so often something happens to erase all sense of difference between you, as on one of those multigenerational *Star Treks* when the old *Enterprise* and the new both show up fifty years apart, at the same quantum singularity, a gateway through time, and Captains Kirk and Picard take each other's measure. There is no future and no past, and they are both in the prime of their lives. There is only ever now, and they each inhabit it.

Like gravitational wormholes in the fabric of the universe, children collapse time and space around themselves. I was standing just behind Sophie for part of the time that she spent reading from the Torah, and her silver yad, its tip formed in the shape of an effete little pointing hand, seemed to career down the column of ancient text, to fly like the thirty-one years gone since the day that I had stood in a dusty-rose three-piece suit with white piping at the lapels, reading from that crazy old rolled-up book of lies, laws, and wonders. We hoisted our prayer shawl higher and swallowed, took a breath, then set off again down the column of Hebrew letters. For an instant, past and future perfectly coincided. She was not rising and I was not setting. Because the lives of a child and a parent are not a pair of counterweights, dragging the hands of a clock around its sorry dial, one rising and the other falling at exactly the same inexorable rate of gears and passing seconds. Or perhaps they are, but if so, it's a process that is happening still, much too slowly for me to see it. All I could see that day for an hour or so, in that high sunny room with a blue-painted ceiling and everyone we love and care about around us, was my wife and my daughter and me, neither passing nor being passed but here together for a while, hanging out in the middle of life.

We are so accustomed to thinking of ourselves, of our lives and histories, in terms of the succession of generations—"Let the word go forth from this time and place . . . that the torch has been passed to a new generation"—that we no longer even question the validity or truth of the idea, which, apart from the most strictly biological sense, has no real meaning and no basis at all in the way we live those lives or experience our histories as they unfold. There is only one time, and one life, and we all share them, and if there is a torch, then it is far too cumbersome and heavy to be passed.

When the dancing began—we started, of course, with a hora—I escorted my daughter to a sturdy chair, and then a bunch of us, young men and old, graceful and ungainly, stout and fit, took hold of the legs and hoisted her up. There were far more of us than chair legs or places to grab them, and yet somehow, lurching and laughing and tripping over our own and one another's feet, we got her up into the air and managed to dance. She tossed and shone like a torch as we carried her around the room, all of us working together to trace our passage across the dance floor, like the silver yad flying along the letters of the oldest story in the world. I looked up at her, grinning and beautiful and terrified and happy, and felt not the same old "time is fleeting and we are all mortal" but something finer and simpler and harder even to bear in mind. This is our life happening, I told her, or would have told her if I could have caught my breath long enough to say it over the clamor of the clarinet and fiddle, and it's happening right *now*.